The West Wing Ultimate Superfan Trivia Challenge!

Scott Robinson

Dedicated to Wingnuts everywhere!

Also by Scott Robinson ...

What's Next?

    The West Wing Guide to American Democracy

    The West Wing Guide to Global Politics

Red Brains, Blue Brains

    The Psychology of MAGA

    Authoritarian We Will Go!

What the Hell...?

    What the Hell is Authoritarianism?

    What the Hell is Neoliberalism?

    What the Hell is Project 2025?

    What the Hell is Christian Nationalism?

    What the Hell is the Oligarchy?

Introduction

People who really love *The West Wing* – well, they *really love The West Wing!*

Like *Star Trek* fans, they buy the DVD box sets and watch the show from start to finish, over and over. Some do an annual viewing, some just watch the show in a continuous cycle. Some watch all seven seasons, some just the Sorkin four.

And there comes a point at which they know every last detail: Leo's middle name; Sam's alma mater; CJ's high school sports achievement; Josh's college roommate; Toby's father's profession. With the loyalty of Who fans, us Wingnuts (yes, I'm a big one) embrace *The West Wing* universe with undying enthusiasm and affection.

Are you a Wingnut, too? Then you might really enjoy gauging your West Wing knowledge with this expansive collection of trivia challenges. See how much you know, and pick up some new tidbits along the way!

STR
July 2024

"Pilot"
S1/E1

The president's bicycle accident becomes an overblown faux crisis; Josh is nearly fired for making an insulting remark to a religious leader on live television; Sam accidentally sleeps with a call girl.

1. What is the make and model of the jetliner Toby is traveling in?
2. How long had that jetliner been in service when Toby was on it?
3. What are the names of the three Religious Right leaders who visit the White House in the episode?
4. What is the name of the granddaughter Jed Bartlet mentions, which of his daughters is her mother, and how old is she?
5. What is the name of the service Laurie works for?
6. How many Cubans set out from Havana to reach Florida? How many turned back? How many were missing or presumed dead? How many did the Coast Guard rescue?
7. Who is Mandy working for?
8. According to Sam, who was the 18th President of the United States?
9. What is the name of the fringe religious group who sent President Bartlet's granddaughter a Raggedy Ann doll with a knife stuck through its throat?
10. What phone number does Sam give his journalist friend Billy to call for info about Josh's possible firing?

"Post Hoc, Ergo Proptor Hoc" S1/E2

The White House hires Mandy Hampton to help manage their public image; the president has a new personal physician; Vice President John Hoynes gets into it with the president over a quote about a gun bill.

1. In confronting Lloyd Russell over his abandonment of his campaign effort, Mandy mentions an Italian opera. Which one?
2. Who is the president's physician in this episode?
3. Josh drinks from the keg of glory; what does he then demand of Donna?
4. Sam tells Toby where he met Laurie (in the previous episode). Where was that?
5. What name does Laurie go by when Sam seeks her out at the restaurant later?
6. Who declined an invitation to the White House?
7. How is the military aircraft transporting the president's physician destroyed?
8. President Bartlet declares that he will blow the attackers off the face of the earth – with what?
9. What does the Latin phrase "post hoc, ergo propter hoc" mean?
10. Where does the president say that phrase is going to appear?

"A Proportional Response" S1/E3

The president's new military physician is killed when a plane he's aboard is shot down, and the president wildly overreacts; Josh hires Charlie Young to be the president's new body man; Sam suffers slings and arrows over this misadventure with Laurie.

1. What does Admiral Fitzwallace call the operation prepared as retaliation for the downing of a military plane in the previous episode?
2. What kind of gun and bullets was Charlie's mother killed by?
3. CJ says Sam is three things that all mean the same thing. What are they?
4. Sam then accuses CJ of not standing up to the "character police" because she lacks three things that all mean the same thing. What are they?
5. Who referred Charlie Young to Josh Lyman for the position of presidential body man?
6. What's the name of the guy who had the job before Charlie?
7. What position is Charlie initially seeking?
8. Where did President Bartlet leave his glasses?
9. What is Charlie's younger sister's name?
10. At this point in the show, how long has Danny Concannon been a White House reporter?

"Five Votes Down"
S1/E4

Leo forgets his anniversary, and his inattention to his marriage has put it at risk; the staff scrambles to secure enough votes to pass a gun control bill; and staff financial disclosures create a headache for Toby.

1. What song is played as President Bartlet finishes his speech? (Sam and Mandy discuss it moments later)
2. How long does the president say he and the first lady have been married?
3. What's the bill being voted on in this episode?
4. What kind of bill is it?
5. What's the name of the freshman representative (whom Josh got elected) that switched his vote on HR 802, causing Josh to say that Congress makes him so sick he could vomit?
6. What is Leo's wife's name?
7. What gift does he buy her for their anniversary?
8. When Jenny leaves Leo, where does she say she'll be staying?
9. Where does Vice President Hoynes' personal AA meeting take place? When? How many does he say are in the group?
10. What two drugs had President Bartlet taken when he showed up high in the Oval Office in a Notre Dame sweatshirt?

"The Crackpots and These Women" S1/E5

Leo makes it a special day for the staff; Josh is briefed on where he should go in the event of a nuclear attack; Toby learns that he was not the president's first choice for White House communications director; and the president hosts a chili supper for everyone in the residence.

1. During the basketball game the president is playing with the staff, it's mentioned that President Bartlet brought in what real-world tennis pro as a ringer in a game of mixed doubles he played with Toby and CJ?
2. It's a special day at the White House, an event created by Leo called what?
3. What is Toby's name for the special day?
4. Bob, who is Sam's first special day appointment, claims to be from what organization?
5. CJ meets with a group that wants to build a wolves-only highway, an 1,800-mile path from Yellowstone to the Yukon. What is the name of the wolf whose story they tell to justify their request?
6. What's the name of Sam's assistant?
7. On the night of the chili party in the residence, where is the First Lady?
8. Who does Charlie meet for the first time in this episode?
9. Charlie is told by the president to relay the message that he does not any additional *what* (spice) added to his chili?
10. What spice does Charlie think the chili needs?

"Mr. Willis of Ohio"
S1/E6

The decennial census is a big issue: Toby and Mandy argue with three Congressional swing votes over the use of statistical sampling in the census as CJ struggles to understand it; the president gets harsh with Leo over his separation from his wife; and Zoey is accosted by three jerks in a Georgetown bar.

1. During the poker game, President Bartlet declares that in the English language, there are three words, and three words only, that begin with the letters *dw*. What are they?
2. Toby refers to Sam by the name of the college he went to. What was it?
3. How much is the US budget surplus that Josh and Donna discuss?
4. What is the name of the head of the president's Secret Service detail?
5. Joe Willis has temporarily taken his deceased wife's seat in Congress. What was her name?
6. What is Mr. Willis's original job?
7. What House bill are Congressmen Willis, Skinner and Gladman discussing with Toby?
8. How many pages long is the bill?
9. What is in the bill that will cause the president to veto it?
10. What local bar does the staff take Charlie out to, what is the drink CJ orders from the bar, and what fake name does Zoey give the three local guys who corner her?

"The State Dinner"
S1/E7

As the White House hosts a state dinner for the president of Indonesia, a hostage crisis is taking place, a major union is threatening to strike, and a hurricane is hitting the Eastern seaboard, threatening an aircraft carrier group.

1. In this episode, a state dinner is given for the president of what nation?
2. A stand-off occurs between a group of survivalists and law enforcement. Where is this standoff?
3. Donna reads up on Indonesia and learns that in certain parts of the country, people are summarily beheaded for being what?
4. What is the name of the hurricane in progress?
5. What is the classification of the hurricane?
6. What union is in the White House at the same as the state dinner takes place, threatening to strike?
7. What is the entree being served at the state dinner?
8. Sam's prostitute friend Laurie is at the state dinner. Who is her date?
9. When the *John F. Kennedy* battle carrier group from Norfolk Navy Yard is moved out to sea to avoid the hurricane but is then caught up in it, what ship does the White House manage to contact?
10. Who does President Bartlet speak to aboard a ship in the carrier group during the hurricane?

"Enemies"
S1/E8

Republicans attach a land use rider to a major banking bill to spite President Bartlet; Mallory sets her eyes on Sam, to Leo's chagrin; the president embarrasses Vice President Hoynes in a Cabinet meeting.

1. Trapped in the Oval Office late at night with the president, Josh calls his boss (with all due respect) a what?
2. What does Leo give his daughter Mallory at breakfast?
3. How much is a cup of coffee at the hotel where Leo is staying?
4. What does Vice President Hoynes tell the cabinet their first priority should be?
5. What does the president tell Hoynes their first priority should be?
6. Mallory asks Sam to go to the opera with her. Who is performing and where?
7. Leo assigns Sam to write a birthday message for who?
8. What does CJ offer Danny Concannon to get him to back off on writing about the president's confrontation of Hoynes at the cabinet meeting?
9. What do Leo and Mallory do instead of going to the opera?
10. Congressmen Eaton and Broderick attach a land use rider to the Banking Bill the White House has been working on passing, to open up Big Sky Federal Reserve for strip mining. What does Josh suggest President Bartlet do to prevent it?

"The Short List"
S1/E9

The staff's choice for a new Supreme Court justice turns out to be ideologically questionable, leading them to consider an alternative; Congressman Lillienfield claims that one in three White House staffers uses drugs; Danny Concannon gives CJ a gift.

1. What is the full name of the Supreme Court nominee the Bartlet Administration initially wants to put forward?
2. What is the name of the Supreme Court justice who is stepping down?
3. To what former president does Justice Crouch compare President Bartlet?
4. What right does Harrison not recognize as constitutional?
5. What was Roberto Mendoza before he was a judge?
6. Which Congressman levels an accusation against the Bartlet Administration in this episode?
7. What is the accusation he makes?
8. What word (predicted by Danny Concannon) appears in every headline on the day following CJ's press conference responding to Lillienfield's accusation?
9. What gift does Danny give CJ in this episode?
10. What is the name of the fake commission Mandy invents to get Mendoza into the White House to see the president?

"In Excelsis Deo"
S1/E10

A homeless man dies of exposure near the Korean War memorial, and Toby is accidentally drawn into it; he proceeds to get involved. President Bartlet does some covert Christmas shopping, as Leo worries about the impact that revelations of his substance abuse history will have on the White House.

1. According to Sam, what record outsold 'White Christmas'?
2. In what Marine battalion did Walter Hufnagel serve in Korea?
3. In what year did his driver's license expire?
4. What is Walter Hufnagel's brother's name?
5. What is Sam's Secret Service codename?
6. What is CJ's Secret Service codename?
7. What book would Josh rather eat than read?
8. What book, considered by President Bartlet as a Christmas gift for Zoey, does Charlie facetiously think she would like better than a new stereo?
9. What is the name of the gay teenager who was killed in this episode?
10. Where were Mrs. Landingham's twin sons killed on Christmas Eve, 1970?

"Lord John Marbury"
S1/E11

A conflict between India and Pakistan heats up quickly, prompting President Bartlet to summon Lord John Marbury, an expert on the region, to the White House for consultation; Josh is subpoenaed with regard to his investigation of drug use in the White House; Zoey dating Charlie makes the president uncomfortable.

1. What new role does Josh want Donna to take up?
2. Which two Eastern nations are in conflict in this episode?
3. How many troops have been deployed along the cease-fire line between them?
4. Who subpoenas Josh?
5. How many lawsuits has Freedom Watch brought against the White House?
6. Leo received substance abuse treatment at what rehab facility?
7. How long was he there in treatment?
8. Lord John Marbury recites the quote from the Book of Revelation that Bartlet cannot remember. What is it?
9. Which Republican Congressman does Mandy want to work for?
10. What actor in what movie does President Bartlet compare himself to when discussing Charlie dating Zoey with Leo?

"He Shall, From Time to Time..."
S1/E12

The staff prepares the president for his second State of the Union address; he collapses in the Oval Office, but is merely diagnosed as having the flu; Abbey reveals to Leo that in fact the president has multiple sclerosis.

1. What are the three typos in the State of the Union teleprompter text?
2. What breaks when President Bartlet collapses in the Oval Office?
3. Who gave the president the thing that breaks?
4. What military doctor treats the president prior to the First Lady's return?
5. What relationship advice does Abbey Bartlet give Leo's daughter Mallory?
6. Josh 'picks a guy'; what for?
7. Who does Josh pick?
8. President Bartlet is presented with a gift by one of his Cabinet secretaries at the end of the episode; what is it?
9. Abbey confides in Leo that the president has a disease. What is it?
10. The president receives regular injections of what, for this disease?

"Take Out the Trash Day"
S1/E13

Leo faces pressure to resign as news of his substance abuse past circulates; the recent murder of a gay teenager prompts the administration to pursue hate-speech legislation; someone in the White House is leaking damage revelations of malfeasance in the vice president's staff; Toby defends PBS.

1. In a previous episode, a teenager named Lowell Lydell was murdered for being gay. His parents appear in this episode. What are their names?
2. What is Josh trying to get Congress to fund?
3. What does Congress want in exchange for the funding?
4. An advance man for the vice president's entourage had the poor judgment to take a Navy helicopter to Pebble Beach to do what?
5. What is the name of the staffer who leaked word of the advance man's malfeasance to the press?
6. Sam tells Toby that a town in Alabama wants to abolish all laws and replace them with what?
7. An old friend of Leo's comes by the White House to urge him to resign, and to let him know that he's written an op-ed piece advocating the resignation for an upcoming edition of the *Washington Post*. What is his name?
8. A Republican congressman speaks to Josh and Sam about avoiding a congressional investigation into a possible cover-up of Leo's past drug and alcohol issues. What is his name?
9. The report Josh wants CJ to read advocates a sex ed concept called "abstinence plus". What was Sam's name for this concept?

10. In his defense of PBS, Toby declares that the administration is going to protect which public television favorites?

"Take This Sabbath Day"
S1/E14

A murderous drug lord is about to be executed, and an old friend of Sam's goads him into trying to persuade President Bartlet to stay the execution; Toby's rabbi gets in on it, delivering a sermon on capital punishment just for him; a political operative from California appears at the White House to give Josh grief about supporting a Congressional candidate.

1. What is the name of Sam's old friend who calls him to try and stay an execution in this episode?
2. What is the name of the prisoner who is going to be executed?
3. For what crime(s) is he being executed?
4. What is the prisoner's mother's name?
5. What is Toby's rabbi's name?
6. What political operative, gifted in polling and statistics, debuts in this episode?
7. What is this operative's assistant's name?
8. This political operative is running a campaign for a Congressional candidate for the California 46th. What is the candidate's name?
9. What does President Bartlet call this candidate?
10. What is the name of the clergyman President Bartlet sends for?

"Celestial Navigation"
S1/E15

SCOTUS Justice-to-be Roberto Mendoza is arrested in a small town in Connecticut; Sam and Toby are dispatched to intervene. Josh makes an appearance at a college lecture series, and tells White House anecdotes including a ruckus caused by an insulting comment made by the HUD secretary and his own misadventure of briefing the press corps.

1. What was Roberto Mendoza arrested for?
2. Why did he refuse to cooperate with the police?
3. Where is Mendoza being held?
4. Which Cabinet secretary gets a rebuke from Leo for insulting a congressman, and what are they secretary of?
5. Which congressman does she insult?
6. Why does CJ have to miss the press briefing?
7. What White House initiative does Josh accidentally allude to when the press gang up on him in the briefing?
8. What is the name and rank of the officer who arrested Mendoza?
9. What medical condition does Mendoza have that precludes intoxication?
10. What were the Mendozas doing in Connecticut?

"20 Hours in LA"
S1/E16

The president and staff fly to Southern California to attend a celebrity-rich Democratic fundraising event at the home of a studio mogul; a flag-burning amendment is much discussed; the vice president is pressured to support controversial legislation that he doesn't believe in.

1. Why do President Bartlet and the staff travel to Los Angeles in this episode?
2. Who is hosting the event?
3. What famous real-world celebrities attend the event?
4. A political strategist recommends that the president "sew up re-election right now" by coming out in favor of a Constitutional amendment. What is the strategist's name?
5. What would the proposed amendment do?
6. According to Toby, the political strategist isn't Satan; he's who instead?
7. The White House is pressuring Vice President Hoynes to support what controversial legislation?
8. President Bartlet crashes his daughter Zoey's lunch at what Santa Monica restaurant?
9. What does Sam say is special about the restaurant?
10. A new special agent of the Secret Service on Zoey Bartlet's protection detail meets the president for the first time aboard Air Force One in this episode. What is her name, where did she go to school, and how long did she train for the assignment?

"The White House Pro Am"
S1/E17

President Bartlet and Abbey find themselves at odds when their staffs are out of sync, and when her choice of replacement for a recently-deceased Federal Reserve chairman turns out to be an old boyfriend; a congresswoman threatens to sink an important bill with a fatal rider; Charlie becomes angry when he's told he can't attend a public event with Zoey because of death threats.

1. What is the name of the First Lady's chief of staff?
2. What is the name of the Federal Reserve chairman who died?
3. How long did he serve in that post?
4. Who is expected to replace the deceased fed chairman?
5. Before their confrontation in the Oval Office, Abbey Bartlet calls her husband two pet names. What are they?
6. A member of Congress sees Sam in the gym and mentions their intention to attach a child labor restrictions rider to the trade bill the White House is promoting, which will likely sink it. What is their name?
7. Donna talks about a book she's been reading. What is the book about?
8. Abbey speaks to the member of Congress threatening to attach the rider to the bill at a White House event hosting what group?
9. Danny Concannon's name for that group is what?
10. To apologize for abandoning Zoey at a diner, Charlie brings her a book and three other items. What is the book, and what are the other items?

"Six Meetings Before Lunch"
S1/E18

A White House civil rights attorney nominee causes controversy as an advocate of slavery reparations; Mallory and Sam get into an extended argument; a panda bear dies in the National Zoo.

1. The White House has nominated someone to be the new Assistant Attorney General for Civil Rights. What is his name?
2. The nominee is controversial because of a quote of his that appears on the dust jacket of a new book. What is the name of the book?
3. The book and the quote are about slavery reparations, which the nominee supports. How much does he say the descendants of slaves are owed?
4. Mallory and Sam spend the episode arguing. What about?
5. CJ performs a lip-sync song. What is the song?
6. Zoey gets caught lying, covering for a friend who is arrested at a frat party she attends. What is the friend's name?
7. What is the name of the journalist who accosts Zoey?
8. Mandy talks to Toby about a panda bear that died in the National Zoo. What was the bear's name?
9. CJ asks for Sam's advice in dealing with the president regarding the problem with Zoey and the press. What is Sam's advice?
10. The president relaxes on a sofa in the Oval Office with a book, *Rules of Civility and Decent Behavior in Company and Conversation*. Who wrote it?

"Let Bartlet Be Bartlet"
S1/E19

An embarrassing memo is circulating among the press corps; Sam tries to talk "Don't Ask, Don't Tell" with military representatives; two resignations prompt the president to investigating reform on the commission resigned from; Leo confronts the president about his inert performance in office.

1. What criticism does Mrs. Landingham make of the president's diet?
2. There's a "piece of paper" floating around the press corps. What is it?
3. Who wrote it?
4. In this episode, two commissioners resign from what commission?
5. The staff wants the president to nominate two reform-minded candidates to the commission. Who are they?
6. How much does Charlie make per week?
7. According to CNN/USA Today, where is the Bartlet Administration's job approval rating at this point?
8. In retaliation for nominating reformers to the FEC, Josh predicts that Congressional Republicans will put a controversial issue on the table. Which issue?
9. Sam is meeting with military personnel to discuss possible changes to what policy?
10. Margaret, Leo's assistant, has a technical issue in this episode. What is it?

"Mandatory Minimums"
S1/E20

Toby's ex-wife meets with him to goad him to action on an issue that concerns her; the president's nominees for the commission replacements cause an uproar among Republicans; pollsters descend upon the White House to help the staff prepare for challenges from the Republicans on unpopular issues.

1. Toby's ex-wife appears in this episode. Who is she?
2. What is her job?
3. When Toby meets with her in a park, she offers him something from her picnic lunch. What is it?
4. CJ makes a mistake in her press briefing on the FEC nominations mentioned in the previous episode. What does she do wrong?
5. Toby is bringing in two pollsters to gather statistics he can use to defend against the anticipated Republican retribution over the FEC nominations. Who are the pollsters?
6. What criticism of mandatory minimums does the staff (and Toby's ex) make?
7. When the staff has breakfast at an outdoor cafe on Tuesday morning, what does Donna call Josh's suit?
8. Toby's ex makes a disclosure to him. What is it?
9. Republican Congressional staffer Steve Onorato tries to coax Sam into taking the lead on the administration's new drug policy?
10. Josh takes a phone call from the Senate Majority Leader. He says one thing, then hangs up on him. What does he say?

"Lies, Damn Lies and Statistics" S1/E21

President Bartlet figures out how to get the new FEC reform commissioners he wants; a daisy chain of firing and promotion is set in motion so that Bartlet can get a wayward ambassador home before he publicly embarrasses his family and the White House; the staff makes predictions about their approval rating.

1. President Bartlet meets with a senior Senator who shares his views on election reform, to get support for his FEC nominees. He tells the senator "We agree on nothing," and summarizes the senator's view of him. What is that view?
2. How does the senator summarize Bartlet's view of him?
3. One member of the FEC already in place is actually a closet reformer. Leo finds him out and approaches him for support. What is his name?
4. In this episode, President Bartlet fires the US ambassador to Bulgaria for having an affair with the daughter of that country's prime minister. What is the ambassador's name?
5. What confession does he make to the president upon his firing?
6. In what ocean is the Federated States of Micronesia?
7. The US Embassy in the Federated States of Micronesia is not located on the island of Yap, as many people believe, but elsewhere. Where?
8. What two gifts does Sam give his friend Laurie for graduating law school?
9. Joey Lucas conducts a poll to see where the administration's approval rating stands (it was 42% the previous week). What does CJ predict it will be?
10. What is the actual new approval rating, according to Joey's poll?

"What Kind of Day Has It Been?" S1/E22

Toby's brother is on a space shuttle mission that's in trouble; the president does a town hall meeting with young people; white supremacists attack the presidential entourage.

1. President Bartlet does a town hall meeting in a community near Washington, DC. Where?
2. In the town hall meeting, President Bartlet mentions that his ancestor, Dr. Josiah Bartlet, was a delegate to the Second Continental Congress. What relation was he to the president?
3. Whose baby pictures does the president threaten to break out and show the crowd?
4. What is Toby's brother's name?
5. What are his academic specialties?
6. How many space shuttle missions has he been on?
7. What NASA official is in charge of the mission Toby's brother is on?
8. How many shooters fire on the president and his entourage?
9. What is the name of the US pilot who is shot down over the Iraqi desert?
10. The president finishes the town hall with a profound quote. What is it?

SEASON 1 EPISODE QUIZ ANSWERS

S1E1: "Pilot"
1. Lockheed Eagle series L-1011
2. 20 months
3. Al Caldwell, Mary March, John Van Dyke
4. Annie, Elizabeth, 12
5. Cashmere Escort Service
6. 1,200 / 700 / 350 137
7. Sen. Lloyd Russell
8. Franklin Delano Roosevelt
9. The Lambs of God
10. 1-800-BITE-ME

S1E2: "Post Hoc, Ergo Propter Hoc"
1. *Nesun Dorma*
2. Capt. Morris Tolliver
3. "Bring me the finest muffins and bagels in all the land!"
4. The Four Seasons
5. Brittany
6. The Ryder Cup team
7. With a surface-to-air missile
8. "The fury of God's own thunder"
9. "After it, therefore because of it"
10. On CJ's tombstone

S1E3: "A Proportional Response"
1. Pericles One
2. A Western .38 revolver firing KTWs (Cop Killer Bullets)
3. High profile, very visible, much noticed
4. Strength, guts, courage
5. Debbie DiLaguardia
6. Ted Miller
7. Messenger
8. In his private study in the residence
9. Deena
10. Seven years

S1E4: "Five Votes Down"
1. "Happy Days are Here Again"
2. 32 years
3. House Resolution 802
4. A gun control bill
5. Christopher Wick
6. Jenny
7. A pearl choker
8. The Watergate
9. The OEMB, downstairs office / 11pm / nine
10. Vicodin and Percocet

S1E5: "The Crackpots and These Women"
1. Steffi Graf
2. Big Block of Cheese Day
3. "Throw Open Our Office Doors to People Who Want to Discuss Things We Could Care Less About... Day"
4. United States Space Command
5. Pluie
6. Cathy
7. Pakistan
8. The president's daughter Zoey
9. Cumin
10. Oregano

S1E6: "Mr. Willis of Ohio"
1. *Dwindle, dwarf, dwell*
2. Princeton
3. $32 billion
4. Ron Butterfield
5. Janice
6. 8th grade social studies teacher
7. The Appropriations Bill
8. 7,000
9. An amendment prohibiting the use of sampling in the national decennial census
10. Georgetowne Station, a grasshopper, Cassandra

S1E7: "The State Dinner"

1. Indonesia
2. McClane, Idaho
3. Sorcerers
4. Hurricane Sarah
5. Class 4
6. The Teamsters
7. Salmon
8. Carl Everett, who raised money for the Bartlet campaign in the Midwest
9. The USS Hickory
10. Signalman Third Class Harold Lewis

S1E8: "Enemies"

1. Nerd
2. Opera tickets
3. $6.50
4. Finding a way to work with Congress
5. Finding a way to best serve the American people
6. Beijing Opera, at the Kennedy Center
7. The Assistant Transportation Secretary
8. A 30-minute sit-down interview
9. Coffee and dessert
10. Declare Big Sky a national park

S1E9: "The Short List"

1. Peyton Cabot Harrison III
2. Justice Joseph Crouch
3. Harry Truman
4. The right to privacy
5. A police officer
6. Peter Lillienfield
7. That one in three White House staffers uses drugs
8. Subpoena
9. A goldfish named Gail
10. The President's Commission for Hispanic Opportunity

S1E10: "In Excelsis Deo"

1. 'Feliz Navidad'
2. The Second of the Seventh
3. 1973
4. George
5. 'Princeton'
6. 'Flamingo'
7. *The Adventures of James Capen Adams, Mountaineer and Grizzly Bear Hunter of California*
8. *The Nature of Things: A Viviscalic Poem Translated from the Latin of Titus Lucrecius Carus*
9. Lowell Lydell
10. DaNang, Vietnam

S1E11: "Lord John Marbury"

1. Being his golf caddy
2. India and Pakistan
3. 300,000
4. Claypool, of Freedom Watch
5. 7
6. Sierra Tucson
7. 28 days
8. "And I looked, and I beheld a pale horse, and the name that sat on him was Death, and Hell followed with him."
9. Mike Brace
10. Spencer Tracy in *Guess Who's Coming to Dinner*

S1E12: "He Shall, From Time to Time..."

1. *hallowed* has a # sign in the middle; 321st century; "our country is *stranger* than it was a year ago"
2. A Steuben glass pitcher
3. The Christian Charity Network
4. Admiral Hackett
5. "Don't go for the geniuses; they never want to sleep."

6. A Cabinet secretary (and officer in the presidential line of succession) to skip the State of the Union address in the Capitol; a 'designated survivor'
7. Roger Tribby, Secretary of Agriculture
8. A copy of the US Constitution, translated into Latin
9. Multiple sclerosis
10. Betaseron

S1E13: "Take Out the Trash Day"
1. Jonathon and Jennifer Lydell
2. 100,000 new teachers
3. That public school sex education be limited to abstinence-only content
4. Play golf
5. Karen Larsen
6. The Ten Commandments
7. Simon Blye
8. Joseph Bruno
9. "everything but"
10. The Muppets, Wall Street Week, Live from Lincoln Center and Julia Childs

S1E14: "Take This Sabbath Day"
1. Bobby Zane
2. Simon Cruz
3. Two drug-related murders
4. Sophia
5. Glassman
6. Joey Lucas
7. Kenny Thurman
8. Bill O'Dwyer
9. an "empty shirt"
10. Father Thomas Cavanaugh

S1E15: "Celestial Navigation"
1. drunk driving
2. The breathalyzer test they wanted him to take constituted an illegal search
3. A police station in Wesley, Connecticut
4. Deborah O'Leary, Secretary of Housing and Urban Development
5. Congressman Jack Wooden
6. A trip to the dentist for a root canal
7. A "secret plan to fight inflation"
8. Sgt. McNamara
9. Chronic persistent hepatitis, a non-progressive for of liver inflammation
10. Antiquing

S1E16: "20 Hours in LA"
1. To attend a Democratic fundraiser
2. Ted Marcus, a film studio president
3. David Hasselhoff and Jay Leno
4. Al Kiefer
5. prohibit flag-burning
6. the guy that runs into 7-Eleven to get Satan a pack of cigarettes
7. An ethanol tax credit
8. Playa Cantina
9. "They make the guacamole right in front of you"
10. Gina Toscano; University of Virginia; 18 months

S1E17: "The White House Pro-Am"
1. Lilly Mays
2. Bernie Dahl
3. 11 years
4. Ron Ehrlich
5. Pumpkin, Gumdrop
6. Becky Reeseman
7. What life was like 100 years ago
8. The Michigan Women's Democratic Caucus
9. The Many Women of Michigan

10. Introduction to Advanced Trigonometry; flowers; popcorn; videos

S1E18: "Six Meetings Before Lunch"
1. Jeff Breckenridge
2. *The Unpaid Debt*
3. $1.7 trillion
4. School vouchers
5. "The Jackal"
6. David Arbor
7. Edgar Drumm
8. Lum-Lum
9. "Get in his face"
10. George Washington

S1E19: "Let Bartlet Be Bartlet"
1. He isn't getting enough roughage
2. An opposition research memo on the weaknesses of the Bartlet Administration
3. Mandy
4. The Federal Election Commission
5. John Bacon and Patricia Calhoun
6. $600
7. 42%
8. English as the national language
9. The "Don't Ask, Don't Tell" policy regarding gay people serving in the military
10. The e-mail system is forwarding emails "at subatomic speed", clogging everyone's inboxes

S1E20: "Mandatory Minimums"
1. Andrea Wyatt
2. Maryland Congressionwoman
3. Homemade pie
4. She says the president nominated a Republican and a Democrat to the commission, when he was under no legal obligation to do so (he was)

5. Al Kiefer and Joey Lucas
6. That mandatory minimums are racist
7. His "Joey Lucas suit"
8. That she went out on a date with a baseball executive, and a cop pulled him over for bumping another car, declining to give the executive a blood-alcohol test because recognized her
9. So he can publicly embarrass him over his relationship with a prostitute
10. "Take your legislative agenda and shove it up your ass."

S1E21: "Lies, Damn Lies and Statistics"
1. That he's "a lily-livered, bleeding-heart, liberal egghead communist"
2. He's a "gun-totin' redneck sonofabitch"
3. Barry Haskel
4. Ken Cochran
5. That he never voted for him
6. The Pacific Ocean
7. The state of Pohnpei
8. A pen and a briefcase
9. Five points higher – 47%
10. 51%, a gain of nine points

S1E22: "What Kind of Day Has It Been?"
1. Rosslyn, Virginia
2. His great-grandfather's great-grandfather
3. His daughter Zoey's
4. David Ziegler
5. Biology and physiology
6. 4
7. Peter Jobson
8. 2
9. Captain Scott Hotchkiss
10. "Decisions are made by those who show up."

"In the Shadow of Two Gunmen"
(Part 1)
S2/E1

White supremacists attack the presidential entourage outside the Newseum in Rosslyn after President Bartlet holds a town hall meeting; the president and Josh are injured, Josh critically so; while Josh is in surgery, flashback scenes revisit how the Bartlet staff first came together.

1. Who spotted the shooters and their accomplice first?
2. As the president is being prepped for surgery, Abbey speaks to Dr. Lee, the anesthesiologist; what does she say to him?
3. In flashback, Josh is shown in a meeting with then-Senator John Hoynes and other staffers, discussing an issue Hoynes would rather avoid during the upcoming presidential campaign; what is the issue?
4. In flashback, Leo visits Josh and urges him to go to hear Gov. Jed Bartlet speak; where does this speech take place?
5. Why does Leo say Josh should go hear Bartlet speak?
6. In flashback, Josh in turn visits Sam; where is Sam working at the time?
7. Sam's firm is working on a deal when Josh arrives to see him; what is the deal?
8. What did CJ lose during the attack?
9. In flashback, Toby sits in a tavern idly chatting to a middle-aged woman; he tells her he is a political operative, and when she asks how many elections he's won, what is his answer?
10. As a member of New Hampshire's Congressional delegation, Jed Bartlet voted against a bill that was popular within his constituency; Toby gets in trouble with other campaign

staffers for encouraging Bartlet to tell the truth about his vote. What was the bill?

"In the Shadow of Two Gunmen"
(Part 2)
S2/E2

As Josh's surgery continues, more flashbacks fill in the story of the Bartlet team's origins; the shooters' accomplice is arrested, and reveals an unexpected intention behind the attack; there is confusion about who is in charge of the government while the president is under anesthesia.

1. What is the accomplice's name, and what white supremacist organization did he belong to?
2. Who were the shooters actually shooting at?
3. Who has the thing CJ lost in the attack?
4. In flashback, what new position does Sam on the oil tanker fleet deal when his law firm meets again with the oil company executives?
5. In flashback, CJ is shown in the public relations offices where she worked before joining the Bartlet campaign; what is the name of the firm?
6. In this scene, CJ is confronted by an angry movie mogul whose movies she's been promoting. What is his name?
7. In flashback, Toby is waiting at CJ's house when she returns there after being fired, to offer her the role of press secretary in a future Bartlet Administration and to ask her to join the campaign. How much will she be paid as a campaign staffer?
8. In flashback, Donna Moss crashes the Bartlet campaign and appoints herself Josh's assistant. In telling Josh her story, she reveals that in four years at the University of Wisconsin, she had how many different majors?
9. In flashback, when Bartlet wins the Illinois primary, Josh calls

for the music playing in the room to be replaced. What does he want to hear?
10. In flashback, Josh's father dies on the night of the Illinois primary. What does Josh's father die of?

"The Midterms"
S2/E3

During the first Midterm elections of the Bartlet presidency, the White House backs an old Duke classmate of Sam's who turns out to be too controversial; Toby struggles emotionally in the aftermath of the assassination attempt.

1. While convalescing at home after his surgery, Josh calls CJ to urge her to include mention of a breakthrough in physics regarding the Theory of Everything. What is this theory's formal name (mentioned later by Sam)?
2. What is the name of Sam's old Duke classmate whom he persuades to run for Congress (and what is his wife's name)?
3. An old New Hampshire nemesis of President Bartlet is polling strong in a local school board race back home, which irritates him. What is that old nemesis's name?
4. The White House is forced to abandon its support of Sam's old classmate. Why?
5. In this episode, the White House holds a Talk Radio reception. President Bartlet arrives to say a few words and singles out an Evangelical radio personality. What is this person's name and title?
6. The staff congregates on the steps of Josh's townhouse, where he is still recuperating. What is Josh wearing?
7. The president is showing off by bringing up the word *acalculia*; what does this word mean?
8. Experiencing residual trauma from the assassination attempt, Toby seeks out the president and requests a leave of absence. How long a leave does the president give him?
9. At the Talk Radio reception, the President speculates that the radio personality he confronts might be mistaking the reception for a different event. What event?

10. What is the law that prohibits campaign fundraising on government property?

"In This White House"
S2/E4

Sam appears on a political talk show where he meets Republican political analyst Ainsley Hayes, whom Leo hires; the president of a poor African nation meets with Big Pharma executives to plea for assistance in an AIDS epidemic.

1. What's the name of the television program Sam appears on, and who is its host?
2. The West Coast town of Kirkwood is in what state? What state does Sam think it's in?
3. What country's president attends the White House summit with Big Pharma to discuss AIDS?
4. What is the president's name?
5. At a press conference, the foreign president mentions the name of a real-world American agronomist who saved countless lives in India by developing a new strain of wheat. What is his name?
6. Ainsley Hayes once clerked for a Supreme Court justice; which one?
7. Why does CJ believe she may be in trouble after speaking with a reporter?
8. How does Ainsley describe the White House staff to her Republican friends?
9. In the episode's final scene, President Bartlet mentions a famous real-world book, published in the Sixties, that predicted world-wide famine; Borlaug's wheat discovery refuted the book's premise. What was the book, and who was its author?
10. That final scene takes place on a Saturday morning in Toby's office. What is President Bartlet wearing?

"And It's Surely to Their Credit"
S2/E5

Ainsley Hayes joins the White House staff as an associate in the White House Counsel's office. She receives a shaky welcome as two staffers, in trouble for disrespecting a Congressional committee, take it out on her. Her new boss, White House Counsel Lionel Tribbey, is also none-too-welcoming, but she wins his respect, as Sam comes to her defense. The backdrop for the episode is the musicals of Gilbert & Sullivan.

1. Who is the White House Counsel at this point in the series?
2. Ainsley is given a less-than-posh office; what is the room she's assigned normally called?
3. There's a lot of Gilbert & Sullivan in this episode. According to both Ainsley and Leo, what are all G&S comic operas about?
4. "He is an Englishman" is from which G&S comic opera, according to the White House counsel?
5. Which G&S opera does Ainsley, Toby, Leo and Sam all say that song is from?
6. Two staffers in the Counsel's office gave mistaken testimony to Governmental Affairs, and Ainsley is sent to clean it up. Who are the staffers?
7. In their mistaken testimony, they stated that the White House was not in possession of what document (when it actually was)?
8. Angered at Ainsley's intrusion, the two staffers leave what for her?
9. As President Bartlet tries, without much success, to record his Friday radio address, he says that studio mogul Jack

Warner used to call him by a nickname. What is the nickname?

10. The First Lady has been away in Pennsylvania, dedicating a monument. Who was the monument for?

"The Lame Duck Congress"
S2/E6

The White House considers calling a lame duck session in order to push through a treaty before the new Senate convenes; a Russian reform politician crashes the White House, determined to meet with the president; Donna goes full Norma Rae to bring attention to repetitive stress injuries in the workplace.

1. What is the name of the Russian reform politician who visits the White House?
2. What is the treaty the White House is trying to push through?
3. What is Leo's response when Donna pushes him to implement OSHA's program for dealing with carpal tunnel syndrome?
4. A *Washington Post* editorial says the Bartlet West Wing resembles _____ and compares Leo to a _____?
5. Sam asks Ainsley to summarize a position paper he wrote. What is the position paper about?
6. What does Ainsley do instead?
7. What state is Ainsley from?
8. Where did she get her law degree?
9. What does Ainsley want from Sam in exchange for helping him with his position paper?
10. What does President Bartlet say that he will do to appease CJ's request that he protest the *Washington Post*'s recent editorials?

"The Portland Trip"
S2/E7

During a late-night flight aboard Air Force One, Sam struggles to improve a speech he's written for the president that will be delivered in Portland; new ideas about public education are discussed; Josh meets with a friend in Congress to discuss the Marriage Recognition Act; and the US seizes an oil tanker in the Gulf.

1. Why is the president going to Portland?
2. Why did President Bartlet insist that CJ go on the trip?
3. What else does the president make CJ do?
4. What congressman does Josh meet with?
5. Donna, feeling mocked by Josh, comes up with a new nickname for him. What is it?
6. When CJ recalls Sam's mediocre draft of the education speech, who refuses to surrender it?
7. What is Charlie's idea for incentivizing young people to become teachers?
8. What instruments did Donna and Ainsley play in high school band?
9. What is Josh's recommendation to the president regarding the Marriage Recognition Act?
10. Why is Margaret afraid Leo might drink?

"Shibboleth"
S2/E8

A group of persecuted Christians from China arrive at a West Coast port, hiding in the cargo hold of a ship, challenging the White House to deal with them without upsetting the Chinese government; CJ has to choose which of two Thanksgiving turkeys will be pardoned, rather than eaten.

1. How many Chinese asylum seekers stowed away in the cargo hold? How many died en route?
2. Sam envisions pilgrims who churn butter, worship according to their beliefs, and do what else?
3. CJ must choose which of two turkeys will receive a presidential pardon. What are their names?
4. CJ says in this episode that she has a master's degree. From what school?
5. Charlie's chore is to find something for the president that will meet with his approval. What is it?
6. The president gives Charlie a gift in this episode. What is it?
7. What are Josh, Toby and Sam doing for Thanksgiving?
8. Who does Toby put up for a recess appointment as Assistant Secretary for Primary and Secondary Education? And why?
9. What does the word 'shibboleth' mean?
10. Who does President Bartlet call to arrange the 'escape' of the Chinese asylum seekers from their INS detention?

"Galileo"
S2/E9

An unmanned spacecraft will soon land on Mars, and the president is preparing to host a televised classroom about it; a fire in a Russian oil refinery turns out to be something very different; the press learns that the president does not like green beans, causing Toby and CJ some electoral grief.

1. How many schoolchildren will be watching the president's televised classroom presentation?
2. Josh draws a particularly dull assignment in this episode. What is it?
3. What goes wrong with the Galileo mission?
4. The president calls for a broader theme for the televised classroom event. Who does he ask to work on developing that theme?
5. The president attends a performance at the Kennedy Center. Who is performing?
6. Sam dreads running into Mallory at the event. She has been dating an athlete; what is his sport?
7. How much taxpayer money was spent on the Galileo mission, according to Mallory?
8. What instrument did President Bartlet take lessons for as a child?
9. What claim does CJ make about herself in her chat with Tad Whitney outside the Kennedy Center?
10. What does the Russian oil refinery fire turn out to actually be?

"Noël"
S2/E10

Leo brings in a trauma specialist to work with Josh as he deals with the aftermath of having been shot; an Air Force pilot flies a fighter jet into the side of a mountain; a woman causes a ruckus on the White House tour.

1. What is the name of the therapist who meets with Josh?
2. How does Josh say he injured his hand?
3. What did the Air Force pilot who crashed have in common with Josh?
4. What was the final message sent by the pilot before he crashed?
5. Toby makes some special arrangements in the West Wing lobby in this episode. What for?
6. Josh has an emotional meltdown that signals to Leo that he is in crisis and needs help. Where is he when this meltdown occurs, and who is in the room with him?
7. A woman on the White House tour became very excited and distressed. What caused her distress?
8. What is the name of the staffer from the White House Visitors Office who assists CJ in accommodating the woman?
9. What does CJ call Bernard at the end of their conversation? What does Bernard later call CJ in return?
10. What is the therapist's diagnosis of Josh?

"The Leadership Breakfast"
S2/E11

Toby makes a serious blunder as preparations for a bipartisan leadership breakfast are made, causing headaches for CJ; Sam floats the idea of moving the press corps out of the West Wing and across the street; Leo insults a *New York Times* columnist by making a joke about her shoes; Sam and Josh almost burn down the White House.

1. As the episode opens, Sam and Josh create a fire hazard. How?
2. In creating a seating chart for the leadership breakfast, CJ inadvertently leaves someone out. Who?
3. What frustrates Toby about the plans for the breakfast?
4. What is the name of the chief of staff of the Senate majority leader, with whom Toby has breakfast?
5. What gift does she give Toby at breakfast?
6. Why does Sam think it's a good idea to move the press corps across the street?
7. What is the name of the *New York Times* columnist whose shoes Leo made a joke about?
8. Donna is dispatched to clear up the misunderstanding between Leo and the columnist; what is in the envelope the columnist later sends Donna?
9. What is underneath the White House Press Room?
10. Leo and Toby shake hands in the Oval Office at the end of the episode, forming something. What?

"The Drop-In"
S2/E12

President Bartlet welcomes a procession of new ambassadors from foreign countries; Leo and Lord John Marbury argue over the US military's flailing ABM development program; an admonishment of environmental extremism makes its way into a presidential speech, angering Sam.

1. When Leo drags the president down the Situation Room to watch an ABM test, the president quotes a famous cartoon strip when it fails. What is the cartoon strip, and what is the quote?
2. By how much does the missile miss its target?
3. Environmental extremes have burned down a ski resort as an act of protest to protect what species?
4. CJ proclaims that a real-world pop musician once wrote her a letter. Which one?
5. What does Lord John Marbury call CJ?
6. What does he call Leo?
7. CJ has to dis-invite a comedian from hosting the Will Rogers Dinner. What is the comedian's name?
8. Where is President Bartlet giving his environmental policy speech?
9. Leo and Lord Marbury disagree over what in this episode?
10. How much federal funding has the not-yet-successful NMD system received? What is Josh's suggestion for a better use of the money?

"Bartlet's Third State of the Union" S2/E13

Bartlet delivers his third State of the Union address, after which he must deal with a hostage crisis in Colombia, where five US DEA agents have been taken. As *Capital Beat* broadcasts live from the West Wing, CJ copes with a potential issue surrounding one of the SotU guests, and Ainsley reveals on the air that she has yet to meet the president. Joey Lucas and Donna try to conduct a phone survey as Josh simmers with impatience.

1. What issue does the phone survey concern?
2. Which Republican congressman appears opposite CJ on *Capital Beat*?
3. There are several wardrobe changes that occur; what prompts them?
4. What's the name of the police officer who is recognized by the president at the SotU?
5. What did President Bartlet advocate in his speech that the ACLU representative on Capital Beat objects to?
6. How long has Ainsley been working at the White House on the night of the SofU?
7. What is the codename for the mission to rescue the DEA agents?
8. What does CJ offer Capital Beat host Mark Gottfried in exchange for not mentioning the controversy concerning the SotU guest?
9. There's a check unaccounted for in the Bartlet joint account, one written by the First Lady for a woman in need at a shelter. How much was the check for?
10. Abbey Bartlet is very angry with her husband, because she

has concluded that the contents of the State of the Union address was intended to do what?

"The War at Home"
S2/E14

In the wake of the State of the Union address, the rescue mission to save the five DEA agents in Colombia goes awry, killing nine soldiers; President Bartlet and Abbey are at odds over his intention to run for a second term.

1. Who visits CJ's office in the first few minutes of the episode?
2. What senator wants to meet with Toby?
3. Why is that senator upset?
4. What is the bad-pun punchline of the joke Toby tells about tiny fish getting taught in the tentacles of a predator?
5. Why is Josh so concerned about the results of the gun initiative survey?
6. Donna points out to Josh that if he married Joey Lucas, they would be Josh and Josephine Lymon-Lucas, and that would have what great benefit?
7. President Bartlet notes that he can't smoke in the building, but Ainsley can do what?
8. What does the President of Mexico offer President Bartlet following the deaths of the soldiers sent in to rescue the DEA agents?
9. How was the Blackhawk helicopter carrying the nine soldiers who died taken down in Colombia?
10. Where and when did the bodies of the soldiers who died arrive back on home soil?

"Ellie"
S2/E15

The Surgeon General makes a comment on a webcast saying that marijuana is no more dangerous than alcohol, causing an uproar that threatens her with dismissal; the president's middle daughter, Eleanor – a medical student at nearby Johns Hopkins – follows that up with a statement in the press that her father would never fire the Surgeon General for telling the truth.

1. What is the name of the Surgeon General?
2. During the webcast, the Surgeon General suggests that the boyfriend of an audience member put his bong where?
3. A newspaper ad announces that President Bartlet is one of many prominent public figures who denounced a new movie that a conservative family values group is denouncing. What is the name of the movie?
4. Who is the movie's producer?
5. A number of activist groups want a specific senator appointed to the Blue Ribbon Commission to study Social Security reform. Which senator?
6. When Josh goes to see the Surgeon General, what does he instruct her to do?
7. What does she give him as he leaves her office?
8. Who did Ellie call to make her statement about the Surgeon General?
9. Who gives Toby the idea of appointing Seth Gillette to the Blue Ribbon Commission without telling him?
10. What movie did Charlie choose for the president's movie night instead?

"Somebody's Going to Emergency, Somebody's Going to Jail" S2/E16

It's Big Block of Cheese Day again, and Sam's good deed is to help Donna seek a posthumous pardon for the grandfather of an old classmate, who was convicted in connection with espionage charges decades earlier. Toby's task is to moderate a forum of activists who have issues with the World Trade Organization; Josh and CJ meet with socially-conscious cartographers.

1. Where does this episode's name come from?
2. What has been stressing Sam so much that he's been sleeping on Toby's office couch?
3. What is the organization that the cartographers belong to?
4. What map do they want the president to advocate for use in public school classrooms?
5. What is the name of Donna's old classmate?
6. What is the name of the grandfather who was accused of espionage?
7. Who does Sam visit at the FBI to deliver a heads-up that he intends to recommend that Stephanie's grandfather be pardoned?
8. Who informs Sam that Stephanie's grandfather was, in fact, a spy for the Russians?
9. Who does Sam quote when he gets angry about the grandfather's treason?
10. President Bartlet and Charlie are trying to decide on a building site. For what?

"The Stackhouse Filibuster"
S2/E17

Sen. Howard Stackhouse stages a filibuster to block a vote on a healthcare bill focusing on children's health issues. The filibuster is particularly inconvenient to the White House staff, as they know they have the votes to win and it is Friday night and they want their victory in the weekend news cycle. Along the way, Sam gets "spanked" by an intern; staffers tag up with family members over email; and VP Hoynes oddly steps up to push back in defense of the administration's clean air initiatives, puzzling Toby.

1. What is the name of the healthcare bill?
2. How old is Howard Stackhouse?
3. Who is CJ writing an email to?
4. At one point, CJ mentions how long Stackhouse has been standing in her email. How long has he been standing?
5. What's the name of the intern who "spanks" Sam?
6. How old is she?
7. What's the name of the Energy Secretary?
8. Which classic author of fiction, read by Stackhouse, is Sam's favorite?
9. How many recipes does CJ think there are?
10. Stackhouse is filibustering to have a $47 million amendment added to the bill. What is this amendment for?

"17 People"
S2/E18

Toby figures out why Hoynes stepped up to slap down Big Oil, confronting Leo when he realizes it's because Hoynes thinks the president won't stand for re-election. The staff stays late to work on a speech for the president, with Ainsley lending a hand. Possible terrorist activity has President Bartlet considering closing US airports.

1. The speech the staff is working on is for what event?
2. They are rewriting it for what reason?
3. Ainsley is going to participate in a panel discussion at Smith College, her alma mater. She is in opposition to what famous legislation?
4. What is Ainsley's religious persuasion?
5. Ed and Larry come up with a joke for the speech. What does their joke require?
6. What did Josh give Donna in this episode?
7. Why does the gift annoy Donna?
8. The First Lady will not be at the White House Correspondents' Dinner. Where is she instead?
9. Why did Donna break up with her boyfriend?
10. Who are the 17 people?

"Bad Moon Rising"
S2/E19

Now that Toby has been informed about the president's MS, Leo recommends to the president that they involve the new White House Counsel. As plans for confronting the issue emerge and other staffers are informed, Josh begins focusing on an economic crisis in Mexico. The coastal collision of an oil tanker brings back memories for Sam.

1. What is the name of the new White House Counsel?
2. He has a gavel that means a lot to him. What does his staff call the gavel?
3. Who gave his father the gavel?
4. What does he smash with the gavel?
5. What's the economic crisis in Mexico?
6. The crashed oil tanker belongs to what oil company?
7. Why is Sam troubled by the oil tanker collision?
8. Toby is very angry and letting the world know it. What is he angry about?
9. President Bartlet takes Charlie aside and instructs him never to lie, when questioned by lawyers or investigators in connection with their relationship and his MS. What does he tell Charlie will happen if he does?
10. The White House Counsel instructs Bartlet that there needs to be a three-word response to all challenges, inquisition and attacks in the coming confrontation over his MS announcement. What is the response?

"The Fall's Gonna Kill You"
S2/E20

After being informed of the president's MS, CJ is loath to trust Babish. The staff ponders how to tell the public. Josh seeks out Joey Lucas to covertly gather polling data that might suggest how they can navigate the coming public response will be.

1. A fax from NASA arrives at the White House. What does it say, and who becomes very concerned?
2. What does Josh tell Joey Lucas the survey is going to be about?
3. An administration official meets with Josh to see if the White House can find additional funding for an initiative. What is the initiative?
4. The official says something to Josh as he's leaving that resonates with Josh because it reminds him of Bartlet's MS secrecy. What does he say?
5. A newspaper article calls Toby and Sam the _____ and _____ of speechwriting?
6. According to Toby, which of them is which?
7. The Progressive Caucus wants Sam to add a line to a speech the president is going to give concerning CBO revenue projects that justify a tax reduction for the middle class. Sam refuses; what is the line?
8. Abbey had something named after her. What?
9. Disclosure of the president's MS was omitted from what?
10. At the end of the episode, CJ laughs at Josh, saying he, Leo and the president are concerned about the wrong things. She alludes to two iconic movie characters to make her point: "You all are like _____ and _____". What characters does she reference?

"18th and Potomac"
S2/E21

Joey Lucas proceeds with her covert poll; she returns to the White House, where the results are discussed in a basement war room. As strategy around these results is discussed, a new international crisis emerges with the deposing of Haiti's lawfully elected president in a military coup. Charlie is informed by the DC police that Mrs. Landingham has been killed in a traffic accident; Leo informs the president.

1. What positive result emerged from Joey's poll?
2. What is the name of the Haitian president who was deposed?
3. What color is Mrs. Landingham's new car?
4. What was Mrs. Landingham's husband's name?
5. How is the Haitian president delivered to the US embassy?
6. Donna is the first staffer at the assistants' level to be advised of the president's MS. Who tells her?
7. What three extras for her car do Josh and Charlie ask Mrs. Landingham about?
8. While discussing coverage of an interview with the president to discuss the MS issue with a network news director, CJ is asked by the director if "the water is over her head." What is her reply?
9. What is the basement war room password?
10. Why is Mrs. Landingham returning to the White House on the evening she is killed in the traffic accident?

"Two Cathedrals"
S2/E22

As President Bartlet simultaneously mourns Mrs. Landingham and prepares to publicly announce his intentions regarding running for a second term, he is beset with memories of when he first met her, as a student at the prep school where his father served as headmaster.

1. President Bartlet recalls being introduced to Mrs. Landingham by his father, decades earlier. What is the name of the woman Mrs. Landingham replaced?
2. Leo puts a media executive on Toby's appointment calendar. What is the executive's name, and why does he want to see Toby?
3. Who does the first reading at Mrs. Landingham's funeral?
4. What is the reading?
5. What issue does young Mrs. Landingham raise with young Jed Bartlet while he's hosing down boats on the school grounds?
6. When young Jed asks why young Mrs. Landingham is speaking to him so candidly, what is her response?
7. After the funeral, the president asks for privacy in the cathedral and addresses the Almighty in an angry screed, during which he addresses him with two pejorative terms. What are they?
8. What gesture does Jed Bartlet (young or old) make, when he's made up his mind to do something?
9. Jed Bartlet tries to discuss the school pay disparity with his father, who ends their conversation by slapping his son hard across the face. What does Jed say that triggers his father?
10. As the president and his entourage are making their way to the press conference in the rain, the episode soundtrack features a pop/rock ballad. What is the song and what band is it by?

SEASON 2 EPISODE QUIZ ANSWERS

S2E1: "In the Shadow of Two Gunmen (Part I)"
1. Zoey's Secret Service agent, Gina Toscano
2. She reveals that the president has multiple sclerosis, and says that he can make up his own mind about whether to tell the press
3. Social security reform
4. Nashua, New Hampshire
5. "'Cause that's what sons do for old friends of their fathers."
6. The law firm Gage, Whitney, Pace, in Midtown Manhattan
7. The purchase of a fleet of oil tankers for Kensington Oil
8. Her necklace
9. None, but he expects her to be impressed at his consistency
10. The New England Dairy Farming Compact

S2E2: "In the Shadow of Two Gunmen (Part 2)"
1. Carl LeRoy; West Virginia White Pride
2. Charlie
3. CJ lost her necklace, and Sam has it
4. That they should forget about purchasing the second-rate tankers they are considering, and buy safer ones instead
5. Triton Day, Beverly Hills
6. Roger Becker
7. $600 a week
8. 5: Political Science, Government, Sociology, Psychology, and Biology (with minors in French and Drama)
9. The Doobie Brothers
10. A pulmonary embolism, which caused a fatal heart attack

S2E3: "The Midterms"
1. The Grand Unified Theory
2. Tom Jordan; Sarah
3. Elliot Roush
4. He attended an all-white fraternity in school, and has a prosecutorial record of favoring white jurors for black defendants

5. Dr. Jenna Jacobs
6. Oversized pajamas that CJ gave him
7. An inability to perform arithmetic functions
8. 15 minutes
9. the monthly meeting of the Ignorant Tightass Club
10. The Pendleton Act

S2E4: "In This White House"
1. *Capital Beat*; Mark Gottfried
2. California; Oregon
3. The Republic of Equatorial Kuhndu
4. Nimbala
5. Norman Borlaug
6. Dreifort
7. She revealed that a grand jury investigation was underway; but it was not a problem, since she learned about it from a witness, so it was not a problem
8. "Extraordinarily qualified; their intent is good; their commitment is true; they are righteous, and they are patriots"
9. *The Population Bomb*; Paul Erlich
10. A Notre Dame sweatshirt

S2E5: "And It's Surely to Their Credit"
1. Lionel Tribbey
2. The Steam Pipe Trunk Distribution Venue
3. duty
4. *The Pirates of Penzance*
5. *HMS Pinafore*
6. Steve Joyce, Mark Brookline
7. The Rockland memo
8. A basket of dead flowers with a card that reads BITCH
9. "One-Take Bartlet"
10. Nellie Bly, an American investigative journalist who had herself committed to a mental institution in order to gather information about conditions, which she then wrote about, leading to reforms in the treatment of the mentally ill

S2E6: "The Lame Duck Congress"
1. Vasily Konanov
2. a nuclear test ban treaty
3. "Type slower"
4. a high school yearbook office; a substitute teacher
5. Employee fraud
6. She reverses his position in the paper, then persuades him that he should make a different recommendation to Leo and the president
7. North Carolina
8. Harvard
9. To accompany him to Capitol Hill, where he will take meetings on the test ban treaty
10. Cancel his subscription

S2E7: "The Portland Trip"
1. to deliver an important speech on education
2. as punishment for making fun of Notre Dame
3. wear a Notre Dame baseball cap (he also threatens to make her sing the Notre Dame fight song to the press corps, but it gets set aside)
4. Matt Skinner
5. Deputy Downer
6. Danny Concannon
7. have the federal government subsidize their educations in exchange for several years of service in communities where teachers are needed
8. flute (Donna) and trombone (Ainsley)
9. a pocket veto; that the president put it in a drawer, as a symbolic gesture to the gay community
10. his divorce papers arrived

S2E8: "Shibboleth"
1. 96; 13
2. solve crimes
3. Eric and Troy

4. The University of California at Berkeley
5. a good knife for carving a turkey
6. a knife made by the silversmith Paul Revere
7. watching football
8. Josephine McGarry, Leo's sister; to spur a debate over school prayer
9. it was a password used by the ancient Israelites to identify imposters sent across the River Jordan by their enemies
10. the governor of California

S2E9: "Galileo"
1. 60,000
2. deciding who to put on a commemorative stamp
3. NASA loses the signal from Galileo
4. Sam and CJ
5. The Reykjavik Symphony Orchestra
6. hockey
7. $165 million
8. trombone
9. that she's great in bed
10. a burning missile silo

S2E10: "Noël"
1. Stanley Keyworth
2. by breaking a glass as he was setting it down
3. they shared the same birthday
4. "It wasn't the plane."
5. musicians playing Christmas carols
6. the Oval Office; Leo, Sam, and President Bartlet
7. She saw a painting hanging in the West Wing that belonged to her father
8. Bernard Thatch
9. a snob; "a freakish little woman"
10. He has PTSD – Post-Traumatic Stress Disorder

S2E11: "The Leadership Breakfast"
1. They try to start a fire in a sealed fireplace
2. the president
3. Substantive issues will not be discussed
4. Ann Stark
5. a can of New Hampshire maple syrup
6. It will free up much-needed office space
7. Karen Cahill
8. Donna's underwear, which fell out of her pant leg when they were talking
9. a swimming pool
10. the Committee to Re-Elect the President

S2E12: "The Drop-In"
1. *Peanuts*; "Oh, good grief!"
2. 137 miles
3. a lynx
4. Davy Jones of the Monkees
5. Princepessa
6. Gerald
7. Cornelious (Corey) Sykes
8. At the Global Defense Council (GDC) conference
9. the NMD anti-ballistic missile system the US military is developing
10. $60 billion; give it to North Korea in exchange for them not bombing the US

S2E13: "Bartlet's Third State of the Union"
1. A gun-control initiative
2. Congressman Henry Shallick
3. Sitting in wet paint
4. Jack Sloane
5. School uniforms
6. Three months
7. Cassiopeia
8. An exclusive interview with him
9. $500

10. set up the re-election campaign

S2E14: "The War at Home"
1. Officer Jack Sloane, the controversial State of the Union guest
2. Seth Gillette, the junior senator from North Dakota
3. He is angry about the president's intention to form a bipartisan Blue Ribbon Commission to study Social Security reform
4. "With friends like these, who needs anemones?"
5. Five congressmen are sitting on the fence over the issue
6. They wouldn't have to get their towels re-monogrammed
7. Pee in Leo's closet
8. Release Juan Aguilar from prison
9. With a shoulder-mounted surface-to-air missile
10. Dover Air Force Base, 4 a.m. that morning

S2E15: "Ellie"
1. Dr. Millicent (Millie) Griffith
2. In the closet beyond the Allman Brothers albums, where it belongs
3. *Prince of New York*
4. Morgan Ross
5. Seth Gillette
6. resign
7. a lollipop
8. Danny Concannon
9. His ex-wife, Congresswoman Andrea (Andy) Wyatt
10. *Dial M for Murder*

S2E16: "Somebody's Going to Emergency, Somebody's Going to Jail"
1. "In a New York Minute", by Don Henley
2. He learned that his father has been keeping a lover in an apartment in Santa Monica for 28 years
3. Cartographers for Social Equality
4. The Peters Projection Map
5. Stephanie Gault
6. Daniel Gault

7. Mike Casper
8. NSA Nancy McNally
9. Abraham Lincoln
10. For his presidential library

S2E17: "The Stackhouse Filibuster"
1. The Family Wellness Act
2. 78
3. Her father
4. Eight hours
5. Winifred Hooper
6. 19
7. Bill Trotter
8. Charles Dickens
9. 20 or 30
10. To fight autism

S2E18: "17 People"
1. The White House Correspondents' Dinner
2. It isn't funny
3. The Equal Rights Amendment
4. Episcopalian
5. A John Wayne impersonation and a sock puppet
6. Flowers, in celebration of the anniversary of Donna coming to work for him
7. Because the flowers recognize the date of the second time she came to work for him (and remained), rather than the first time she came to work for him (and left)
8. At the Bartlet's home in Manchester, New Hampshire
9. She was in a car accident and taken to the hospital, and on his way to the hospital to meet her he stopped at a bar to have a beer with friends
10. Abbey Bartlet, the Bartlet daughters, the original doctors and radiologists, the president's brother, Admiral Fitzwallace, VP Hoynes, Leo, Dr. David Lee (the anesthesiologist who treated the president when he was shot), Toby, and the president himself.

S2E19: "Bad Moon Rising"

1. Oliver Babish
2. The Big Hammer
3. Supreme Court Justice Louis Brandeis
4. A hand-held tape recorder
5. Mexico is unable to pay the loans that are immediately due
6. Kensington Oil
7. While with Gage Whitney, he helped put together the deal for Kensington to purchase the tanker (but later had a change of heart, knowing the tanker was sub-standard)
8. A leak to the press from a senior White House official
9. "You're finished with me, you understand?" - Charlie will no longer work for him
10. "Bring it on."

S2E20: "The Fall's Gonna Kill You"

1. A Chinese satellite is going to fall to Earth; Donna fears it will wreak havoc on civilization
2. Sub-surface agricultural products; "Are Americans eating more beets?"
3. The government's case against Big Tobacco
4. "These people perpetrated a fraud against the public."
5. Batman and Robin
6. Toby is Batman, Sam is Robin (to which Sam objects)
7. That the administration wants a real tax cut for working families, while opponents want to help the rich pay for bigger swimming pools and faster private jets
8. A Medevac helicopter
9. the family history section of Zoey Bartlet's college application
10. Butch and Sundance

S2E21: "18th and Potomac"

1. Americans are, in fact, eating more beets
2. Dessaline
3. blue

4. Henry
5. in the trunk of a car
6. Toby
7. tow package, extended service warranty, and subwoofers for the stereo
8. that the water is exactly at her head
9. Sagittarius
10. The president was going to tell her about his MS

S2E22: "Two Cathedrals"
1. Mrs. Tillinghouse
2. Greg Summerhays, who wants to offer Toby the position of news director at the news network he is starting
3. Charlie
4. The Book of Wisdom, Chapter III
5. That the women who work at the school are paid less than the men
6. "Because you never had a big sister and you need one."
7. A son of a bitch and a feckless thug
8. Puts his hands in his pockets, looks away and smiles
9. That the school's literature professor had banned Ray Bradbury's *Fahrenheit 451*, which is a book about banning books
10. "Brothers in Arms", by Dire Straits

"Isaac and Ishmael"
S3/E1

In an episode detached from the normal *West Wing* timeline, a White House lockdown over a possible terrorism threat has a class of high schoolers holed up in the building's mess, as each member of the staff drops by to chat with them about weighty matters. Meanwhile, a West Wing staffer of Middle Eastern origin is suspected of being connected to the threat, and is interrogated by Leo and Secret Service Agent Ron Butterfield. (The episode was written and produced in less than two weeks and presented as a response to the 9/11 attacks.)

1. The visiting students are part of what educational project?
2. When Josh addresses the student and claims that the Executive Branch is the most powerful of the three, the student corrects him. What is the student's name?
3. According to Josh, "Islamic extremism is to Islamic as _____ is to Christianity."
4. What is the name of the staffer detained by Leo and Butterfield?
5. What is it about terrorism that Sam is most struck by?
6. What is Sam's answer to the question, "What do you call a society that has to 'just live everyday life with the idea that the pizza place you're eating in can just blow up without any warning?'"
7. The suspected staffer has a degree that adds to Leo's suspicions, obtained at a prestigious US university. What is the degree, and which university?
8. President Bartlet and the First Lady crash the mess classroom session in search of apples. Abbey explains the conflict between Israel and the Arab world by recalling the Old Testament story of Isaac and Ishmael, who shared a

father. Who was their father?
9. The suspected staff, once cleared, confronts Leo, mentioning that he was one of the presidential entourage at a turning-point event from the first season. Which event?
10. Josh leaves the students with advise on how to resist extremists. What is his advise?

"Manchester, Pt. I"
S3/E2

In flashbacks, President Bartlet and the staff strategize on how to proceed with running for re-election. Sam is bothered that the president has not apologized for his failure to disclose his illness; the president and wife Abbey are in conflict over his exclusion of her from his decision. President Bartlet and Leo ponder the best course of action concerning the US embassy in Haiti, contemplating a military rescue.

1. Who is hired to manage the Bartlet re-election campaign?
2. What are the names of the two political strategists Bruno hires to help out?
3. What is the codename of the rescue mission being planned for the US embassy in Haiti?
4. The rescue mission includes the transfer of deposed Haitian President Dessaline and the Americans in the embassy to what US aircraft carrier?
5. What did Joey Lucas's poll use as a stand-in for the president, on the question of how important those surveyed felt his failure to disclose?
6. What impending FDA announcement threatens to conflict with the president's speech kicking off the campaign, causing Josh concern about losing the news cycle?
7. What is special about the M&M boxes aboard Air Force One?
8. Out of frustration, CJ makes a terrible gaffe in a press briefing, when asked if the president's health concerns make it difficult to focus on the crisis in Haiti, causing an uproar. What did CJ say?
9. What Abenaki name do the Bartlets refer to their remote farm?
10. What does it mean?

"Manchester, Pt. II"
S3/E3

The should-he-or-shouldn't-he-apologize debate continues in flashbacks of the President and staff, along with Bruno and his team, at the Bartlet farm in New Hampshire. CJ, still reeling from her press conference gaffe, attempts to resign; the President continues to work toward a peaceful settlement to the crisis in Haiti.

1. As the President and staff work on speech language in the barn, CJ sees a snake and is alarmed. The president dismisses it as harmless, identifying it as what kind of snake?
2. Doug states that Americans want a "happy warrior" to lead the nation, not _____.
3. Bruno wanted his deal to include 15% of the campaign ad buys; what did he have to settle for?
4. At the campaign announcement event, Toby is making corrections to a stack of posters that say BARTLET FOR PRESIDENT. What is Toby revising them to say?
5. Bruno sits privately with Josh and tells him he had recently made a huge strategic mistake that might have helped the campaign? What was the mistake?
6. President Bartlet and Abbey are in their White House bedroom when she offers to take up their long-delayed discussion. He declines, because he is studying something. What is he studying?
7. Who introduced President Bartlet at the campaign announcement?
8. The staff and Bruno's people note an uncommon word in the speech. What is the word?
9. What does it mean?
10. Speaking to the staff and Bruno's team before he goes out to give his speech, he cites two historical figures who were

"serious men using big words for big purpose." Who were they?

"Ways and Means"
S3/E4

CJ gets cagey with the press to have the special prosecutor investigating the President replaced. The President deals with the political fallout of refusing to act to extinguish a Wyoming forest fire, on the advice of scientists, and must decide whether or not to support a repeal of the estate tax. Meanwhile, Donna goes on a blind date with a Republican.

1. What's another name for the estate tax?
2. Where in Wyoming is the forest fire?
3. Who is the Republican that Donna meets for a blind date?
4. Who set her up on the blind date?
5. Donna's Republican date is an attorney. What Congressional committee does he work for?
6. Sam flies out to California with Connie in tow to meet with the head of the American Federation of Service Employees, meaning he can deliver lots of votes. What is his name?
7. Sam wanted to be a fireman when he was four years old. What did Josh want to be when he was four years old?
8. CJ drops a hint to the press that Special Prosecutor Clement Rollins might be too chummy with the Bartlet Administration by casually mentioning that he co-wrote a paper with a current member of the administration while in law school. Who did he co-write the paper with?
9. What is the staff's recommendation to the President regarding the estate tax?
10. CJ makes the argument to Leo that the administration needs to be investigated "by someone who wants to kill us just to watch us die. We need someone perceived by the American people to be irresponsible, untrustworthy, partisan, ambitious, and thirsty for the limelight." Who is she talking about?

"On the Day Before"
S3/E5

On the eve of a State Department dinner, President Bartlet vetoes the estate tax bill, and the staff fears the House of Representatives will override the veto, delivering a serious political blow to the administration; they scramble to deal with Democratic congressmen who want favors in exchange for their votes to block the veto. Josh deals with a possible competitor for the Democratic nomination for president as CJ deals with an entertainment reporter who annoys her with a shallow put-down.

1. What is the name of the Democratic politician who is contemplating a challenge to President Bartlet for the nomination?
2. What office does he hold?
3. Why is the White House staff concerned about the challenge?
4. What does Josh offer him to back down?
5. Who is the entertainment reporter who gets on CJ's bad side?
6. What does she call CJ, on the air, to inspire CJ's retribution?
7. In the wheeling and dealing for the votes of Democratic congressmen looking for handouts, a deal is put together including grazing fees, farm nets and milk subsidies. Sam has the idea of offering that deal to a Republican, to send the message that it's not cool to blackmail the President. What Republican do they offer it to?
8. What term does Leo use to describe this maneuver?
9. Royce asks for one more thing, in exchange for the votes he'll bring. What is it?
10. Charlie is offered immunity for his cooperation in the

investigation of the President, and the staff encourage him to take it. Finally, in response to Leo, he makes a statement of loyalty to end the discussion. What does he say?

"War Crimes"
S3/E6

Leo has a difficult encounter with an old friend from his military days, debating the US's position regarding the War Crimes Tribunal, as President Bartlet pushes a reluctant Vice President Hoynes to address an anti-gun rally in his home state of Texas, where it won't go down well. Donna is called before the Congressional committee investigating the MS scandal. Sam tries to rationalize the penny.

1. What old friend (with whom he served in Vietnam) does Leo meet with?
2. Donna testifies before the committee investigating the President. What day is it?
3. Who is questioning her?
4. Donna lies to the committee – about what?
5. What event motivates President Bartlet to ask Hoynes to go speak at the anti-gun rally in Texas?
6. What is the name of the journalist who returns to the White House briefing room after a long overseas absence and sits in the San Francisco Chronicle's assigned seat?
7. This journalist has a quote about the upcoming election, attributed to Toby, that would be embarrassing to the administration if published. He repeats the quote to CJ and asks if she wants to comment. What is the quote?
8. A Congressional aide meets with Sam to discuss a new bill, the Legal Tender Modernization Act. What does this act call for?
9. Toby meets with the entire communications staff to give them a stern talking-to about leaking embarrassing information to the press. Where does this meeting take place?
10. In their discussion of the War Crimes Tribunal, the general

tells Leo something about their wartime activity that horrifies him. What is it?

"Gone Quiet"
S3/E7

An American submarine goes silent while spying on North Korea off its coast, causing the President to turn to a long-serving assistant Secretary of State for consultation as he contemplates a rescue mission. Abbey learns that her medical past might cause problems in the Congressional investigation of the President's MS scandal, as Toby copes with a Congressional attempt to divert funding from avant garde artists.

1. What is the name of the Assistant Secretary of State who advises the President?
2. He joined the State Department during which presidential administration?
3. What is the name of the missing submarine?
4. Tawny Cryer of the Congressional Appropriations Committee meets with Toby over the redirection of some money to the National Park Service; the intent is to de-fund the National Endowment for the Arts to provide that money. How much money is it?
5. CJ is ecstatic that the Majority Leader got "the question" from the press, and bungled the answer – until she realizes the President himself doesn't have an answer prepared. What is the question?
6. The Assistant Secretary, realizing he will be in the Oval Office for a while, accepts the offer of a soft drink. What does he ask for?
7. What is Leo's advice on how to handle the crisis of the missing submarine (which the President repeats later in the Situation Room)?
8. Where was President Bartlet about to go on Marine One when Leo stopped him because of the submarine incident?

9. Why was he going there?
10. Why does Tawny Cryer want the National Park Service to have the money?

"The Indians in the Lobby"
S3/E8

As President Bartlet ponders Thanksgiving options, CJ is confronted with the problem of two Native Americans who are standing in the West Wing lobby, where the press will see them if they make a scene, holding out for an audience to discuss public health programs on their reservation. Meanwhile, Josh works to get a teenage boy extradited from Europe to face the consequences of killing his teacher, as Sam deals with a revised poverty income index that reclassifying millions of the nation's poor.

1. How old is the teenager who killed his teacher?
2. What state (which now wants him extradited to stand trial) did the murder occur in?
3. From what European country does that state want him extradited?
4. What agency produced the new poverty formula that Sam is dealing with?
5. How many more people will be below the new poverty line than before?
6. What tribe are the Native Americans from?
7. As President Bartlet contemplates preparing the stuffing for his Thanksgiving turkey, Charlie suggests a resource that could help him. What is it?
8. Josh speaks to a foreign ambassador's aide who is trying to find an American children's book. What is the book?
9. Where does President Bartlet *not* want to spend Thanksgiving?
10. Having caught Abbey as the culprit behind the Thanksgiving locale change, he says, *"J'accuse, mon petite fromage!"* What does *"mon petite fromage"* mean?

"H. Con-172"
S3/E11

The Congressional Oversight Committee offers Leo a deal that will end the investigation – a Presidential censure. Leo angrily rejects the offer. Josh awkwardly maintains contact with Amy Gardner as the staff hands around a tell-all book written about them by a temporary staffer. Charlie gives the President an 18th century map of Palestine, but neither CJ nor Toby will allow it to be publicly displayed.

1. What question has Leo been asking his entire adult life?
2. What year was the map of Palestine made?
3. Toby mentions President Bartlet's favorite movie had been on television the night before. What movie is that? (It is not explicitly named in the episode, but it is precisely quoted.)
4. Toby voices one of the quotes, by Prince Richard, which the President then completes: "When the fall is all that's left..." How does the quote end?
5. Where does Amy go on her date before meeting Josh?
6. With whom does Donna have a clandestine meeting in the Federal Case Law section of the Georgetown Law Library?
7. What topic does Josh offer as pretext for his meeting with Amy?
8. Regarding the tell-all book, President Bartlet refuses to talk to Sam about what?
9. How long has Toby's mom been dead?
10. Amy is waiting for Josh on the steps of his apartment building. As they are speaking, she mentions that they didn't talk much in college, and he says it's because she was having "quite a bit of sex" with his roommate. What was the roommate's name?

"100,000 Airplanes"
S3/E12

It's State of the Union time again, and preparations are shown in flashback amid scenes of Sam uncomfortably shadowed during the event itself by his ex-girlfriend, who is writing a magazine feature about him. Josh's pursuit of Amy Gardner continues, as he belittles her relationship with a congressman as a political manipulation. Joey Lucas returns to analyze the responses to the President's SotU address.

1. What is Sam's ex-fianceé's name?
2. What magazine is she writing for?
3. What does "100,000 airplanes" refer to?
4. How many airplanes were originally anticipated?
5. What great initiative, inspired by dinner guests of the Bartlets, was omitted from the State of the Union address?
6. CJ asks about a reason why Sam and his ex- fianceé didn't get married. What is the reason?
7. What does Sam tell Toby the real reason was?
8. What's the name of the congressman Amy is seeing?
9. Angry over Josh's insinuation that the congressman is only dating her as a political maneuver, Amy lists four assets that make her desirable. What are they?
10. Sam reveals to CJ that one issue between he and his ex-fianceé when they were a couple is that he is supposed to know the difference between _____ and _____.

"The Two Bartlets"
S3/E13

The President and his staff are all over the place, as they try to figure out what to do about public comments from Florida Gov. Rob Ritchie, a possible Republican contender for the presidency; Josh plans a tropical getaway with Amy Gardner but has his plans interrupted when he's asked to intervene in a protest involving an old friend of his that is blocking military training exercises; Donna wants out of jury duty; and Sam must deal with his old friend Bob, the UFO nut, who is now demanding an investigation of gold bullion he claims is missing from Ft. Knox.

1. Josh, beginning his morning routine, recycles something. What?
2. Amy Gardner shows up before Josh had even had breakfast. She tells him she received a marriage proposal. From who?
3. After Amy leaves, the phone rings, and Josh begins rattling off a list of their recent romantic encounters. Who is on the other end of the phone?
4. Who is overhearing the call?
5. Speaking of calls, who does CJ talk with on the phone from Air Force Once?
6. CJ tells Toby that they have an opportunity to attend a 4-H convention where they could see several sculptures made out of butter. What sculptures does she mention?
7. Gov. Ritchie's statements are concerning to Toby and he asks Sam to write up some notes to be added to an upcoming speech by the President to push back. What was Ritchie speaking out against?
8. Amy declares in a speech that every two years, the American people get to do what?

9. According to Bob the UFO Nut, which two American presidents have toured the gold vault at Ft. Knox?

10. What does Josh do for Amy to make up for delaying his Tahitian getaway with her?

"Night Five"
S3/E14

President Bartlet has had great difficulty sleeping, and someone is called in to help him with the problem. One of CJ's White House reporters has been taken hostage overseas, and she does all she can to help secure his release. Donna is offered a better-paying job in the private sector, and Sam asks Ainsley for an assist on a proposed bill regarding payment of UN dues. Toby gets in hot water with Andy, once again.

1. Who arrives at the White House, in clandestine fashion, to help President Bartlet with his sleeping disorder?
2. Staffers ask him about his flight, and keep repeating one question in particular. What is it?
3. In what country is CJ's reporter being detained?
4. What compliment does Sam pay Ainsley, who is very attractively attired, that offends a nearby female bullpen staffer?
5. Donna is offered the position of Issues Director for a political website. When she is shown her annual salary, what does she mistakenly take it to be?
6. Toby has written a foreign policy speech that is aggressive, even incendiary. Though the staff loves it, it makes someone else very angry. Who?
7. What does Toby do to placate them?
8. The President expresses distaste for the term "stress", calling it a "Madison Avenue word", something that can be cured with _____ and _____.
9. What does it turn out has been keeping President Bartlet up at night?
10. What happens to CJ's reporter being held hostage in the Congo?

"Hartsfield's Landing"
S3/E15

The voting in the town of Hartsfield's Landing, New Hampshire, has accurately predicted the winner of every presidential primary contest in the state for decades – so Josh is very interested in how that election, which takes place just after midnight on the day of the primary. While he sweats it out, President Bartlet is engaged in tense brinkmanship, playing Red Rover with the Chinese over war games in the Taiwan Strait – while playing chess with Toby and Sam at the same time, in separate rooms. CJ and Charlie get into it over the latter's attempts to police the President's daily schedule.

1. Hartsfield's Landing's run of accurate predictions goes all the way back to the election of which US president?
2. That president founded what great American tradition?
3. How many registered voters are there in Hartsfield's Landing?
4. Where are the two chess games played?
5. What is Charlie's new rule concerning the President's daily schedule, and why did he implement it?
6. What's the name of the family in Hartsfield's Landing that's planning to vote for Ritchie?
7. What does Josh do about it?
8. How does Donna protect herself from the elements?
9. Who gave the chess sets to President Bartlet?
10. What does President Bartlet predict that Sam will one day do?

"Dead Irish Writers"
S3/E16

On the eve of Abbey's birthday, the President arranges a huge surprise to distract her from the impending loss of her medical license. The British Ambassador is in attendance, and proceeds to argue with Toby against the President meeting with an Irish terrorist. Sam is visited by his old physics professor, who lobbies him to fight for federal investment in a very expensive research project. Abbey, CJ, Donna and Amy steal away from the party to privately share some wine, and Donna discovers she is no longer a US citizen.

1. Who is the British Ambassador at this point?
2. What is the name of the Irish terrorist whose presence in the White House he objects to?
3. What compliment does he pay to Abbey?
4. What is Sam's old physics professor's name?
5. What does he want the federal government to build?
6. What senator has put an anonymous hold on the project?
7. The professor is dying? What of?
8. The President tells Charlie that Britain's House of Stuart gave the world the term 'toast', used today to offer a sentiment while raising a drink in the air. What habit of the Stuarts prompted the invention of the term?
9. Amy gets up in Josh's face at Abbey's party. What about?
10. What must Donna do to recover her citizenship?

"The U.S. Poet Laureate"
S3/E17

On live air, President Bartlet says something he shouldn't (as we all do, from time to time) about his Republican opponent, prompting CJ to do some containment. A new US poet laureate has been named and is about to be received at a White House dinner, but she is intent on protesting the refusal of the US to sign onto a land mines treaty – prompting Toby to try to sway her. A tech giant falters, prompting Leo and the President to debate government intervention on their behalf - and Josh discovers there's a website dedicated to him.

1. What is the name of the new poet laureate?
2. What is the name of the website dedicated to Josh?
3. Who does Sam recall from vacation to help deal with the President's on-air gaffe?
4. What did President Bartlet say about Gov. Ritchie on live air that causes the controversy?
5. Which two colleges did President Bartlet attend?
6. What has Tabitha Fortis been thinking a lot about, prior to meeting Toby?
7. Which land mines are at issue in the US position over the treaty?
8. What does she receive in exchange for her agreement not to voice her grievances at the dinner in her honor?
9. After the President's on-air comment about his opponent and CJ's casual dismissal of it, the press begins seeking out what information about Gov. Ritchie?
10. When CJ realizes the President make the "slip" about Ritchie on live air on purpose, she admires it, and calls it what?

"Stirred"
S3/E18

The President handles a crisis caused by the crash of a truck hauling spent uranium fuel rods in a remote highway tunnel, as quiet discussion is undertaken by the staff to consider dropping Vice President Hoynes from the ticket. Hoynes, meanwhile, is trying to keep alive a bill that will provide Internet access to the poor. The President finds time to horn in on Charlie's tax return prep, much to the latter's chagrin, as Donna lobbies Josh for a presidential proclamation honoring her favorite teacher on the occasion of her retirement.

1. In what Western state does the truck with the fuel rods crash?
2. What is the name of Donna's retiring teacher?
3. The President cannot give the teacher a presidential proclamation; what does he do instead?
4. What is Charlie's adjusted gross income?
5. Who is considered as a replacement for Hoynes on the ticket?
6. Why is the rural Internet bill being held up?
7. Leo informs Hoynes that he needs to tell the President something sensitive. What is it?
8. What is Hoynes' reaction?
9. The President writes down his reason for keeping Hoynes on the ticket on a piece of paper. What does it say?
10. What gifts does the President give Charlie as acknowledgment of his pre-tax generosity?

"Enemies Foreign and Domestic"
S3/E19

CJ makes an incendiary comment to the press corps about an incident in the Middle East where 17 schoolgirls were forced to die in a burning building because they weren't wearing the correct clothing. As the President is preparing, with Sam's help, for a summit with this Russian counterpart, he is shows satellite photos of a facility for manufacturing nuclear weapons in Iran, with Russian support. Toby confronts a Russian journalist over press credentials, and Charlie tracks down the source of an inexplicable letter addressed to the President.

1. The letter writer heard a Presidential speech in what city?
2. The President borrowed his private mail code from which of his predecessors?
3. What year was the letter mailed?
4. The Russian working with Sam on the summit preparations slip Sam a speech insert that expresses the futility of nuclear arms escalation, claiming to have written it themselves. Who actually wrote it?
5. The negotiators speak competent conversational English, but they lack... what?
6. What is the name of the computer company that's in trouble?
7. Leo wants to back a loan to help Antares. The President says no, but does something better. What does he do?
8. What do the satellite pictures show?
9. Mr. Tatum, who sent the letter to the President using the private mail code, served as a railroad man for 53 years aboard what famous train?
10. A special Secret Service agent is assigned to protect CJ. What is his name?

"The Black Vera Wang"
S3/E20

An impending terrorist attack is the President's priority as election season looms. Toby finds himself wrestling with recalcitrant network executives who have come to see convention coverage as a loser; CJ, under threat, gets to know the Secret Service assigned to her as she bristles against the protection.

1. CJ, simultaneously annoyed by and enamored with Simon Donovan, calls him "Agent _____". Agent what?
2. Donovan corrects her: what is his correction?
3. Where do Donovan and CJ go on their first trip beyond the White House, and why?
4. What is CJ's niece's name?
5. How long has Donovan been in the Secret Service?
6. A terrorist group developed a plan to blow up what US landmark?
7. What is the name of the Qumari Defense Minister?
8. What gift does Josh bring Donna from the Helsinki trip?
9. What old friend, now part of the Ritchie campaign, does Sam have lunch with?
10. What does Sam give his old friend at the lunch?

"We Killed Yamamato"
S3/E21

US intelligence sources have determined that Qumari Defense Minister Abdul Shareef is in fact a Bahji terrorist leader, and the mastermind behind the attempt to blow up the Golden Gate Bridge. As the President and Leo work with others in the Situation Room to figure out what to do about it, Josh and Amy Gardner squabble over a welfare reform bills, as Sam – having been burned by the campaign videotape – deals with ecological intervention in the Everglades. Donna travels to North Dakota in Josh's place to attend a hearing addressing changing the state's name, and CJ deals with the constant presence of Special Agent Simon Donovan.

1. What city does Josh send Donna to?
2. What name change is North Dakota seeking?
3. Josh has a Sunday meeting that takes him back into the office, interrupting his off-day with Amy. What is the meeting about?
4. According to Amy, all women count on Josh and find him _____.
5. What proposed change to the Welfare Reform Bill, which Josh agrees to as a matter of compromise, infuriates Amy?
6. What show is the President and his entourage planning on attending in New York City?
7. CJ and Simon Donovan go somewhere together after work. Where?
8. What do they do there?
9. Charlie undertakes a long-overdue search. For what?
10. Who persuades Leo to persuade the President that the best course of action regarding Abdul Shareef is to assassinate him?

"Posse Comitatus"
S3/E22

President Bartlet and his entourage attend a Broadway play, where he runs into his Republican rival, Florida Gov. Rob Ritchie. As the play is underway, the plan to assassinate Abdul Shareef unfolds. Josh and Amy are at odds over the Welfare Reform Bill, Charlie finds a replacement for Mrs. Landingham, and Simon Donovan insists on accompanying CJ to the Broadway play, where things go horribly wrong.

1. President Bartlet sits in a private discussion with someone and almost discloses his intention to have Shareef killed. Who is he sitting with?
2. How long is "The War of the Roses"?
3. Simon Donovan is on the street outside the theater talking to CJ when word arrives that her stalker has been captured. Where does he go after they part?
4. What happens there?
5. Per Admiral Fitzwallace's advice, who does President Bartlet have Leo notify of his order to kill Shareef?
6. Where is Shareef assassinated?
7. After receiving word of Donovan's death, President Bartlet runs into Gov. Ritchie in the theater lobby. He tells Ritchie what happened. What is Ritchie's response?
8. What is Bartlet's response to Ritchie's response?
9. Who does Charlie find to replace Mrs. Landingham?
10. The candidate Charlie finds was previously fired from the White House? For what?

SEASON 3 EPISODE QUIZ ANSWERS

S3E1: "Isaac and Ishmael"
1. Presidential Classroom
2. Billy (Fernandez)
3. The KKK
4. Raqim Ali
5. It has a 100% failure rate
6. Israel
7. An applied mathematics degree from MIT
8. Abraham
9. The attempted assassination at Rosslyn, Virginia
10. To remember pluralism, and keep accepting more than one idea

S3E2: "Manchester, Pt. I"
1. Bruno Gianelli
2. Doug (Wegland) and Connie (Tate)
3. Operation Swift Fury
4. The *USS Enterprise*
5. A hypothetical Governor of Michigan, with a degenerative disease
6. The agency's approval of RU-486, a birth control pill
7. They have the seal of the President
8. that the President "is relieved to be focusing on something that matters."
9. "Awasiwi Odinack"
10. "beyond the village", or "far from the things of man"

S3E3: "Manchester, Pt. II"
1. a garter snake
2. Dr. Kevorkian
3. 12%
4. BARTLET IS THE PRESIDENT
5. Issuing the admonition of Big Tobacco prematurely
6. Agriculture
7. Abbey

8. torpor
9. apathy
10. Churchill and FDR

S3E4: "Ways and Means"
1. Death tax
2. Yellowstone National Park
3. Cliff Calley
4. Ainsley
5. When the date is set up, he works for Ways and Means; but he is traded to House Government oversight
6. Victor Campos
7. a ballerina (but he doesn't like to talk about it)
8. White House Counsel Oliver Babish
9. that he threaten to veto any repeal of the tax
10. the US House of Representatives

S3E5: "On the Day Before"
1. Jack Buckland
2. Governor of Indiana
3. He is an award-winning athlete whose health might make the president look bad
4. a place on the short list for Labor Secretary
5. Sherri Wexler
6. a clothes horse
7. Congressman Robert Royce
8. "throwing an elbow"
9. that there be no serious challenge for his seat from the Democrats in the next election
10. "I stay with my team."

S3E6: "War Crimes"
1. USAF Lt. Gen. Alan Adamle
2. Sunday
3. Cliff Calley
4. She claims not to keep a diary, when in fact she does

5. A church shooting with fatalities that has just occurred there
6. Will Sawyer
7. "If the President wins re-election, it will be on the Vice President's coattails."
8. The elimination of the penny
9. The White House mess
10. That a bombing mission Leo flew in Thailand in 1966 struck a civilian target, not a military one, killing 11 innocents

S3E7: "Gone Quiet"
1. Albie Duncan
2. Since the Truman Administration
3. The *USS Portland*
4. $105 million
5. Why does he want to be president?
6. Schweppes' Bitter Lemon on ice, with a twist
7. "Trust the captain, trust the crew."
8. New Hampshire
9. To personally file as a candidate for president, to get on the state's ballot
10. To bolster national park security

S3E8: "The Indians in the Lobby"
1. 13
2. Georgia
3. Italy
4. The Office of Management and Budget (OMB)
5. 4 million
6. Muncie
7. The Butterball Hotline
8. *The Little Red Lighthouse (and the Great Gray Bridge)*
9. Camp David
10. "My little cheese"

S3E9: "The Women of Qumar"
1. Amy Gardner

2. making balloon animals
3. the 60th anniversary of Pearl Harbor
4. The Rotarians and the Elks
5. CJ
6. Red tape, hence the common term for cumbersome bureaucracy
7. "You wanna get hit over the head."
8. a water balloon
9. the Celtics
10. unfunded mandates

S3E10: "Bartlet for America"
1. Cliff Calley, the attorney who had interviewed Donna
2. 32 years
3. 11 years
4. Jordan Kendall
5. "New Hampshire – It's what's new!"
6. Mrs. Landingham
7. Mike Casper
8. the front window of the store they are using as an office
9. that Leo had fallen off the wagon and gotten drunk
10. Cliff Calley

S3E11: "H. Con-172"
1. "How long does it take to get a purse together?"
2. 1709
3. *The Lion in Winter*
4. "...it matters a great deal."
5. the ballet
6. Cliff Calley
7. paid family leave
8. his underwear
9. 12 years
10. Chris

S3E12: "100,000 Airplanes"
1. Lisa Sherbourne

2. *Vanity Fair*
3. the number of military aircraft built by the US during World War II
4. 50,000
5. a call to cure cancer in 10 years
6. that her name would be Lisa Sherbourne Seaborn
7. John Tandy
8. She didn't like him very much
9. wit, charm, brains, and legs that go all the way down to the floor, my friend
10. substance and flash

S3E13: "The Two Bartlets"
1. yesterday's coffee grounds
2. Amy; Congressman John Tandy
3. Leo
4. Margaret
5. her father
6. a butter bow, a butter Elvis, a butter Last Supper
7. affirmative action
8. overthrow the government
9. Roosevelt and Truman
10. decks his apartment out in Tahitian style

S3E14: "Night Five"
1. Dr. Stanley Keyworth
2. if he knew anyone on the plane
3. The Congo
4. "You could make a good dog break his leash."
5. the website's operating budget
6. his ex-wive, Congresswoman Andrea Wyatt
7. He agrees to consider including some notes she offers that contain softer language for the speech
8. flavored coffee and bath bubbles
9. a rough conversation with Toby, in which Toby asked him if his father ever hit him
10. He was killed in an ambush in the Congo

S3E15: "Hartsfield's Landing"

1. William Howard Taft
2. Baseball's 7th Inning Stretch
3. 42
4. The game with Toby is in the Oval Office; the game with Sam is in Sam's office
5. The schedule must be checked out, because it has been frequently leaked to the press room
6. Flender
7. sends Donna out into the cold night to call them by cell phone and talk them out of it
8. takes Josh's coat
9. The Prime Minister of India
10. run for president

S3E16: "Dead Irish Writers"

1. Lord John Marbury
2. Brendan McGann
3. "Your breasts are magnificent!"
4. Dalton Millgate
5. a superconducting supercollider
6. Sen. Jack Enlow
7. Non-Hodgkins Lymphoma
8. putting a piece of toast into a glass of wine to improve its flavor
9. no women are under consideration for the post of Deputy Policy Director
10. pass a three-part literacy test and an American history exam, and fill out a one-page form

S3E17: "The US Poet Laureate"

1. Tabitha Fortis
2. LemonLyman.com
3. Ainsley
4. that he might be "a .22 calibre mind in a .357 Magnum world"
5. Notre Dame and the London School of Economics
6. nothing rhymes with Ziegler

7. about a million land mines in the DMZ between North and South Korea
8. a private meeting with the President so she can tell him her story
9. his college transcripts
10. "old school"

S3E18: "Stirred"
1. Idaho
2. Molly Morello
3. calls her personally, along with Donna, from the Oval Office
4. $35,000 per annum
5. Admiral Fitzwallace
6. to get the Vice President's name off the bill, so the President will not be able to campaign on it
7. that Hoynes is an alcoholic
8. that Leo hadn't already told him
9. "Because I could die"
10. A new DVD player and the DVD *On Her Majesty's Secret Service*

S3E19: "Enemies Foreign and Domestic"
1. Pittsburgh
2. Franklin Roosevelt
3. 1932
4. Newly-elected Russian President Chigorin
5. idioms
6. Antares
7. that the federal government will remain Antares' biggest customer
8. a heavy water reactor, used for making plutonium
9. *The Spirit of St. Louis*
10. Simon Donovan

S3E20: "The Black Vera Wang"
1. Agent Sunshine
2. Special Agent Sunshine
3. to a mall, to buy a junior prom dress for CJ's niece

4. Hogan
5. 9 years
6. the Golden Gate Bridge
7. Abdul Shareef
8. a decorate crate of moose meat
9. Kevin Kahn
10. a video of a negative campaign ad anonymously delivered to Sam

S3E21: "We Killed Yamamato"
1. Bismarck
2. Drop the "North", and just be "Dakota"
3. re-authorizing the Welfare Reform Bill
4. "god-like"
5. the addition of $300 million for "marriage incentives"
6. The War of the Roses
7. the Secret Service gym
8. Simon takes CJ to the gym's firing range, where she shoots a gun and falls over
9. a new executive secretary, to replace Mrs. Landingham
10. Admiral Fitzwallace

S3E22: "Posse Comitatus"
1. Dr. Stanley Keyworth, the therapist who helped him with his sleeping disorder
2. Five and a half hours
3. a convenience store near the theater
4. he is shot and killed while intervening in an armed robbery
5. the Gang of Eight (Congressional leadership and ranking personnel in Intelligence)
6. on an RAF airstrip in Bermuda
7. "Crime... boy, I don't know."
8. "In the future, if you're wondering - 'Crime... boy, I don't know' is when I decided to kick your ass."
9. Deborah Fiderer
10. she was the one who initially hired Charlie

"20 Hours in America, Pt. I"
S4/E1

On the campaign trail in Indiana, Josh, Toby and Donna find themselves left behind when the presidential motorcade pulls out of a small town without them, leaving them to fend for themselves among rural Republicans. Leo discusses the cover-up of Shareef's assassination with Fitzwallace. Aboard Air Force One on the way back to Washington, the President interviews possible replacements for Mrs. Landingham as Bruno and CJ discuss campaign-trail comments by Gov. Ritchie's wife. Sam, grabbing some sleep after several non-stop days, is awakened by Josh, who because of his protracted stay in Indiana asks that Sam staff the President.

1. What's the name of the young woman Toby and Josh talk to in the fields nearby the President's address in Indiana?
2. What's the name of the teenager who drives Josh, Toby and Donna around in a jeep?
3. What do they order at the roadside diner, on the recommendation of the cook?
4. Sam asks if there exists a "Reader's Digest index of all human knowledge." What source does Ginger suggest instead?
5. While waiting for a ride outside a roadside store, Josh and Toby toss rocks into a barrel from a distance, making a bet about who misses first. What must the loser do?
6. Simon Donovan was in the Big Brothers program before he was killed. CJ is seeking a male staffer to fill that role with the young man Simon was Big Brother to. Who is that young man?
7. Sam staffs the President as a fill-in for Josh. Uncertain of how to comport himself, the President advised him to do

what?

8. Republican women voters stage a protest in Madison, Wisconsin with aprons and rolling pins. What are they protesting?

9. Margaret is policing Leo's diet. What does he tell her he had for breakfast?

10. A young Congressman visits the Oval Office for a formal welcome and photo op with the President. What's his name, and how old is he?

"20 Hours in America, Pt. II"
S4/E1

A stock market crisis makes President Bartlet skittish about invoking bad luck, as he ponders what he should do. Sam staffs the President as Josh asked him to, but notices that the ongoing interviews with potential replacements for Mrs. Landingham include questions about the applicants' memories, a possible MS concern. Still trapped in Indiana, Toby, Josh and Donna are delivered to the train by Tyler, but once they board, they find themselves headed in the wrong direction. When they reach civilization, they hear that a bombing has killed students at a university, and Josh and Toby meet a dad in a bar who talks about finding the money to pay for his daughter's college tuition.

1. What action does President Bartlet avoid, with Charlie's superstitious collusion, to fend off bad luck regarding the stock market crisis?
2. Who does Sam see back at the office, after the President's speech?
3. This person calls Sam by a nickname. What is it?
4. Still without a Big Brother, a listless and angry Anthony calls CJ a terrible name. What is it?
5. Someone puts him into a wall for it. Who?
6. What does the President predict that the displaced Josh and Toby would have had to do, had Donna not been with them?
7. Who becomes President Bartlet's new executive secretary?
8. Which of the staff is "in her corner"?
9. What's the name of the man Toby meets in the hotel bar?
10. What university did he and his daughter come out to look at?

"College Kids"
S4/E2

Motivated by their bar chat with citizen-dad Matt Kelley, Josh and Toby conceive a plan to help Americans pay for college, as the President and Leo work on approaches to dealing with possible fallout from Shareef's assassination. Josh and Amy continue to have problems, as Debbie Fiderer has to deal with wrinkles in assuming her new position.

1. President Bartlet tells a story in the Situation Room of his daughter being asked by a teacher why there has always been conflict in the Middle East. The teacher rejected Ellie's answer and provided his own. What was it?
2. How many people died in the pipe bombing?
3. What outside counsel does Leo recruit to assist with the Qumari investigation problem?
4. Who is the agent communicating with the White House on the FBI's investigation of the pipe bombing?
5. Charlie speaks to Debbie Fiderer about a problematic response she made on a security form, tied to a comment she made about the President in the past that could threaten her eligibility for the executive secretary positions. What was the comment?
6. Who is planning to run as a third-party candidate in the presidential election?
7. President Bartlet is unconcerned over Debbie Fiderer's security issue, telling her, "You knock me out!" What did she do that knocks him out?
8. What political operative is working for Howard Stackhouse?
9. Toby quotes something the President said during their first campaign: "There are two kinds of politicians: " What are they?

10. Gov. Ritchie publicly states that he thinks a long-established piece of (real-world) legislation should be re-examined. What it is?

"The Red Mass"
S4/E3

Amy's support of Howard Stackhouse's third-party candidacy causes friction with Josh, as the President deals with a domestic terrorist crisis in Idaho and the staff haggles with Gov. Ritchie's campaign over the number of presidential debates. Leo meets with an Israeli official to discuss fallout from Qumar over the assassination of Shareef.

1. How many debates does the Bartlet campaign want?
2. How many debates will the Ritchie campaign agree to?
3. The Bartlet campaign wants a change in the debate format. What do they want the debate format to be?
4. What do they offer the Ritchie campaign for their agreement to this change in format?
5. What is the Red Mass?
6. What is Anthony's problem with the Red Mass (which he gets up in Charlie's face about)?
7. Sam is informed that someone has just had a heart attack. Who?
8. Why is this of particular importance to Sam?
9. Sen. Stackhouse says to Josh (much to Amy's amusement), "No, Josh, you of all people shouldn't..." What?
10. As Stackhouse agrees to drop out of the campaign, the President decides to take questions from the press on a touchy issue that's important to Stackhouse. What is it?

"Debate Camp"
S4/E4

The President and staff clear a weekend to prepare for the upcoming debate with Gov. Ritchie, simultaneously dealing with an Israeli air strike on Qumar. In flashback, mistakes made during the Bartlet Administration transition are relived, a botched Attorney General nomination in particular, as well as an embarrassing moment for Donna. Toby and Andy, divorced, nonetheless consider having a baby.

1. In the mock debate, who is playing Gov. Ritchie?
2. During the campaign, the President's nominee for Attorney General fell through. Who was he?
3. Why was he dropped from consideration?
4. Donna meets her predecessor, who casually mentions that taking the iodine pills is a matter of personal choice. When Donna asks why anyone would take iodine pills, what does he tell her?
5. While Rooker is under consideration, one staffer in unsupportive of his nomination. Which one?
6. What happens to tip the staff to Rooker's attitude about racial profiling?
7. What Evangelical list does CJ end up on?
8. In a flashback, Mrs. Landingham is selecting loaner art from the National Gallery and the Smithsonian. What does the President want to borrow?
9. In the present, Toby makes an announcement to Josh, Charlie, Sam and CJ. What is it?
10. Bartlet tells Sam that someone has died. Who?

"Game On"
S4/E5

After extensive preparation, President Bartlet debates Gov. Ritchie – and his necktie apparently makes all the difference. State department Republican Albie Duncan assists CJ by providing post-debate spin for the press. In the meantime, Sam deals with the death of Horton Wilde, who was running for Congress in his home district of Orange County, California – where the Wilde campaign is still underway, despite his death, under the leadership of young political operative Will Bailey. He also tells Wilde's widow that if her deceased actually wins, he will stand in for him.

1. Assistant Secretary of State Albie Duncan, who has worked in the State Department for uncountable decades, has a reputation for being crazy. What is Toby's defense of him, when questioned about that?
2. What does Abbey do to motivate her husband, just before the debate begins?
3. What does Sam ask Will Bailey to do, when he arrives at Horton Wilde's campaign headquarters?
4. Why does he ask this?
5. What is Will Bailey's step-sister's name?
6. Toby spontaneously names his unborn twins. What does he name them?
7. Seeking to counter Ritchie's penchant for simplicity, the staff begins seeking what kind of answer?
8. Charlie is obsessed with the President's choice of necktie. Why?
9. Ellie Bartlet's age is stated at one point. What is it?
10. The staff has a private nickname for the President when he's off his game. What is it?

"Election Night"
S4/E6

The contest between President Bartlet and Gov. Ritchie finally comes to a head as America votes. The staff anxiously tracks the vote, as Sam focuses on the voting in the California 47th, where Horton Wilde amasses many votes despite being dead.

1. Which Bartlet staffer always votes early on election day?
2. On this particular election day, that staffer is besieged by voters who have voted incorrectly, to vex him. It's a prank; who is the prankster?
3. What did Toby do in preparation for election night that Sam considers superfluous?
4. Had Toby not done that thing, what did he fear tempting?
5. Toby and Josh demand a penance from Sam for questioning Toby's actions?
6. CJ shares a private concern with Toby that could be bad PR and might need some remediation. What is it?
7. Horton Wilde leads his opponent in Orange County. What act of God helps his campaign along?
8. Why does Debbie deny Josh entry into the Oval Office for the Senior Staff meeting?
9. Charlie hosts Anthony and a football player from Anthony's school, then takes the latter out to do something he's never done. What?
10. Donna meets Navy Cmdr. Jack Reese outside the polls, and implores him to do her a favor. What is it?

"Process Stories"
S4/E7

The President and First Lady retire to the residence to celebrate the election victory in private as the staff copes with a wave of unexpected incidents. Sam is now on the hook as Orange County stand-in for the departed Horton Wilde, and wrestles with whether or not to follow through with his commitment. CJ wants Bruno to take a bow, and wants a boastful campaign wannabe to stop taking them.

1. How does word break that Sam will be standing in for Horton Wilde?
2. What real-world news anchor calls the White House to see if the President is endorsing Sam?
3. Toby goes to Andy's victory party and asks her to do what?
4. A Midwest pollster is running around the West Wing celebration, taking credit for much of the Bartlet campaign strategy, drawing CJ's ire. What is his name?
5. Why did Amy come to the West Wing victory party?
6. Donna runs into Navy Lt. Cmdr. Jack Reese at the party. What is he doing at the White House?
7. He breaks something in her presence to make a point. What?
8. How much was the broken thing worth?
9. Who interrupts the President and First Lady as they're trying to get busy?
10. What song are staffers singing in CJ's office?

"Swiss Diplomacy"
S4/E8

The son of the Iranian Ayatollah needs life-saving surgery immediately, and only the United States can provide it. The Ayatollah reaches out in secret for help, while publicly railing against the infidels. The White House is ethically compelled to do everything possible to save the boy's life, which sucking it up in the face of the criticism. Toby tries to offer a compensatory administration position to a Congresswoman who martyred her seat in a good cause. Sam begins his Congressional campaign in California. Toby's ex-wife, Congresswoman Andrea Wyatt, faces a lawsuit.

1. What is the operation the Ayatollah's son needs to survive?
2. Such an operation has only been successfully done in the US, but one other country is working on it. What country?
3. A Congresswoman who has just been voted out visits Toby in his office. What is her name?
4. Toby offers her a new job. What is it?
5. Andy is about to be sued. What for?
6. Sam, beginning his campaign for the California 47th, becomes upset with Will Bailey. What about?
7. The President refers to a Mrs. Wilburforce, from the family's past. Who does he think that is?
8. Who was Mrs. Wilburforce actually?
9. A Congressman complains to Josh that someone is already shopping precinct campaigns for the next election. Who does Josh accuse of doing this?
10. Who is the one actually doing it?

"Arctic Radar"
S4/E9

Stymied in his effort to get Will Bailey to run his Congressional campaign, Sam instead maneuvers him Toby's direction to get him onto the White House staff as a speechwriter. A reporter in CJ's press room is upset about her seating assignments.

1. CJ informs the President that a Navy pilot has been arrested. What is the pilot's name?
2. Why was the pilot arrested?
3. The President meets with his cabinet to congratulate them on a great first term, listing some of their successes. After he leaves the room, Leo addresses them all. What does he ask of them?
4. What is the reporter who argues with CJ upset about?
5. Josh objects to something a staffer is wearing. What is it?
6. Donna asks Josh for a favor. What is the favor?
7. The pilot who's in trouble had two prominent first-ever accomplishments in Navy history. What were they?
8. Leo persuades Charlie to deflect an angry phone call from the President. Who is the phone call from?
9. What are they calling about?
10. Sam gave Will a note to give to Toby. What does the note say?

"Holy Night"
S4/E10

A flashback takes us back to the Fifties, where Toby's father is an unwitting ride-along on a murder. Unaware of what is transpiring, he excitedly tells his colleagues about his newborn son Tobias.

In the present, Toby is surprised by the appearance of his father at the White House, and surprised further still to find Josh is behind the visit. His day is further ruined by a deposition he must give. A snowstorm hitting Washington hard weighs the evening down.

1. What is the name of the vocal group singing in the West Wing?
2. Toby is deposed by Freedom Watch. What about?
3. Someone long missing crashes CJ's final pre-Christmas briefing dressed as Santa. Who is it?
4. What is Toby's father's name?
5. What song are the Whiffenpoofs singing to Donna in the Mural Room?
6. What did Toby's father do for a living?
7. And what did he do for that?
8. What story is Danny Concannon working on now?
9. Zoey is dating someone new. What is his name and nationality?
10. Zoey asks for her father's permission. What for?

"Guns Not Butter"
S4/E11

A foreign aid bill has come before the Senate and the White House staff finds itself fighting to get it passed. The President has a photo op with an animal, and Charlie is passed an envelope by a woman on a rope line that leads to conversations with the military.

1. Josh argues with a Republican staffer over the political challenge of foreign aid. What is that challenge?
2. Why did Charlie and Zoey break up?
3. There is a meeting with an animal on the President's schedule. What animal?
4. That animal turns out to be a different animal. What kind?
5. Danny shares the latest on his story of Shareef's death with CJ, mentioning that he is investigating Jamil Bari, the pilot who flew Shareef's plane the night he was assassination. What has Danny concluded about the pilot?
6. What is the nature of the letter handed to Charlie by the woman on the rope line?
7. Josh has Donna and others lying in wait in various locations, including an airport, for an elusive senator. Why?
8. A senator meets with Toby, offering to switch his vote on the foreign aid bill in exchange for $115,000 to fund a study. What is the study?
9. According to Will, what famous politician said that the best argument against democracy is five minutes with the average voter?
10. What did that famous politician also say?

"The Long Goodbye"
S4/E12

CJ returns to her hometown to speak at her high school class reunion, confronting a deteriorating situation with her father, who has Alzheimer's Disease. Back in the West Wing, Toby scrambles as he tries to cover for her.

1. Where does CJ go (where is she from)?
2. What is her father's name?
3. What was his job, before he retired?
4. What classmate does CJ run into, and subsequently hook up with?
5. What unusual skill does he reveal?
6. He was a punk rocker in high school. What was the name of his band?
7. What is the title of CJ's speech to her high school class?
8. CJ's father remarried, giving her a stepmother. What is her stepmother's name?
9. CJ's father, dementia aside, recalls her classmate's hairstyle in his high school days. What was it?
10. What does CJ's father give the classmate as he is departing?

"Inauguration, Pt. I"
S4/E13

Faraway events compel the staff to re-write the President's Inaugural address at the eleventh hour, to include a bold and controversial new doctrine (one that gets the administration in hot water with the Pentagon). A genocide in the Republic of Equatorial Kundu stir the President's conscience, egged on by Will Bailey. Danny Concannon gets ever closer to learning what really happened to Abdul Shareef.

1. How many Inaugural balls must the President attend?
2. What is missing from the Inauguration, causing Charlie to go into a mad scramble?
3. Lt. Cmdr. Jack Reese is suddenly no longer assigned to the White House. Why not?
4. Leo and the President are concerned about the Chief Justice. What is their concern?
5. There is a terrible crisis in an African nation. Which one?
6. What is happening there that causes the White House great alarm?
7. When President Bartlet privately says to Will Bailey, rhetorically, "Why is a Kundunese life worth less to me than an American life?", what is Will's reply?
8. The President comments on Will's reply. What does he say about it?
9. How many buttons are there on the trousers of a Navy dress uniform?
10. According to the force depletion report covertly submitted to the President, what are the estimated troop losses for a US military intervention in Kundu?

"Inauguration: Over There"
S4/E14

As the situation in Kundu grows increasingly dire, the President resolves to introduce a new doctrine, to be announced in his Inaugural address. Someone in the West Wing leaks a negative quote to the *Washington Post* that triggers a search for the leaker.

1. What is Will's father's name, rank, and former posting?
2. What did President Bartlet give his daughters when they were young, behind Abbey's back?
3. What is the new doctrine the President wants to announce and adopt?
4. What does he see on late-night television that gives him the idea for the new doctrine?
5. Who does CJ suspect of being the leaker?
6. Who is the actual leaker?
7. What major decision regarding Will does Toby make?
8. Josh, Danny, Charlie, Will and Toby venture to Donna's apartment in a cab to drag her to the Inaugural balls. Josh has deduced something she did in secret, and accuses her. What?
9. If Sam returns from California, he will be promoted. To what?
10. The buzzer outside Donna's apartment doesn't work. How do Josh and the others outside get her attention?

"The California 47th"
S4/E15

The President and staff travel to California to campaign for Sam as they debate when to announce a controversial new tax plan that could be damaging to him. The situation in Kundu grows worse, and the President takes military action, per his new doctrine.

1. What is the name of Sam's campaign manager?
2. How does Debbie Fiderer describe the President's wit?
3. What do the Congressional Republicans do to upset the President's plans for his new tax proposals?
4. The staff argues that responding to the Republican announcement by immediately unveiling their own tax plan will kill Sam's campaign. Why?
5. Three of Will's speechwriting interns have the same first name. What is it?
6. Donna has her picture taken with a former California Gubernatorial candidate named Izzy Perez, and this causes controversy. Why?
7. CJ recommends a change in Sam's campaign. What is it?
8. Toby and Charlie get into a fight with two men in a bar lounge. What is the fight about?
9. Sam becomes very perturbed with the President and staff. Why?
10. What does Sam ask of the audience when he's introducing the President to his audience at a campaign event?

"Red Haven's on Fire"
S4/E16

As US military personnel intervene to stop the slaughter in Kundu, several US troops are captured and President Bartlet authorizes a mission to rescue them. Toby does his best for Sam in his race to win the California 47th as Josh runs afoul with Abbey Bartlet.

1. How many US troops are taken hostage?
2. What does Josh do to irritate the First Lady?
3. What is the name of the First Lady's chief of staff?
4. He is related to her. How?
5. Who becomes the First Lady's new chief of staff?
6. Admiral Fitzwallace corrects the President on the meaning of the term 'wet team', describing the unit that will carry out the hostage rescue mission. Why is that term used?
7. Amy Gardner, along with others, is sitting at the head table at a fundraising luncheon where Abbey Bartlet is speaking from a podium. What does Amy Gardner accidentally do while the First Lady is speaking?
8. Three of Will's four speechwriting interns are named Lauren. What is the fourth one's name?
9. What does 'Red Haven' refer to?
10. How many are killed in the retaliatory strike on the training camp after the hostages are rescued?

"Privateers"
S4/E17

The Daughters of the American Revolution are set to get a new member, but at the same time they are questioning the fitness of Abbey Bartlet, who has been a member for a long time, to remain. An old classmate of Toby's works for a chemical company and turns whistle-blower, asking Toby for help. And Abbey finds herself in the position of opposing her husband when an anti-abortion rider gets attached to a foreign aid bill.

1. Zoey is the latest in a long line of Bartlet women to be admitted to what historic organization?
2. Why is the First Lady's membership being questioned?
3. What's the name of the senator who attached the anti-abortion rider to the foreign aid bill?
4. It's Amy Gardner's first day as the First Lady's chief of staff, and some of the West Wing staffers give her a hazing. What do they make happen?
5. What's the name of Toby's old roommate?
6. What's the name of the White House counsel who interviews him?
7. What is the name of the DAR member that CJ, Will and Amy meet with in the Mural Room?
8. Where is she from?
9. Off the top of her head, Amy comes up with a fake award to be presented to this woman at the DAR ceremony. What is the name of the award?
10. Abbey and Amy Gardner go way back. What did Abbey used to do for her?

"Angel Maintenance"
S4/E18

The President, Charlie, CJ, Will Bailey, Ed, Larry, and a testy press corps are trapped aboard Air Force One after a very long flight from the Far East, due to an indicator light that suggests the plane's landing gear is not locked down, causing CJ and Will to scheme ways to deceive the press about why they won't land. Back at the White House, Josh works with a Republican Congressman on an ecological project.

1. Where are they flying from?
2. A midnight deadline must be dealt with. What is the deadline?
3. What must happen to meet the deadline?
4. Who facilitates that event?
5. Will concocts an excuse to give the press. What is it?
6. He even gives his excuse a fancy technical name. What is it?
7. One of the reporters has news of the conflict in Kundu. What is it?
8. What is the ecological project Josh is working on?
9. Toby visits a Congressman to inform him that one of the soldiers killed by friendly fire in Kundu was a constituent of his. Which Congressman is it?
10. Speculating on her own obituary, Donna gets her own name wrong to underscore her insignificance. What does she call herself?

"Evidence of Things Not Seen" S4/E19

The White House staff's late-night poker game is interrupted when a gunman fires shots at the White House, triggering a lockdown. President Bartlet works to negotiate the return of a US spy plane that has gone down on the Russian coast; Josh interviews a potential replacement for Ainsley Hayes.

1. What's the name of the lawyer Josh is interviewing?
2. The candidate won't sign a form Josh wants him to sign. Why not?
3. What does CJ believe you can do with an egg during an equinox?
4. Why does Will appear at the card game in military uniform?
5. Toby and Will go to the press room to engage in a competition. What is the competition?
6. How many shots are fired at the White House?
7. Where is Will headed?
8. Why is he going there?
9. Zoey gives Charlie some news about her summer plans that doesn't make him happy. What is it?
10. What does Leo threaten to do if Russia insists on retrieving the downed spy plane?

"Life on Mars"
S4/E20

On his first day as Associate White House counsel, Joe Quincy stumbles across two press leaks that seem related: a science editor's inquiry about a suppressed report about a meteor from Mars, and backroom details about a settlement in an anti-trust case. Putting two and two together, he figures out how the leak came about – and the answer is scandalous to the Bartlet Administration.

1. What derogatory term is the staff trying to get Quincy to say?
2. Margaret says that the girls in Political Affairs covered Quincy's parking spot with what?
3. Where is Quincy's West Wing office?
4. What is the name of the *Washington Post*'s new gossip columnist?
5. Quincy figures out who the leaker is. Who is it?
6. The leaker has been having an affair with a person prominent in Washington society. What is their name?
7. Toby writes some notes that go to CJ's desk in which he compares a federal judge to what?
8. Toby is eating a salad and not enjoying it. He tells Charlie that even if he covered it with barbecue sauce, it would still taste like what?
9. How does Quincy tie the White House leaker to the person they are having an affair with?
10. While Quincy is doing his detective work, Will is meeting with his speechwriting interns, working on what?

"Commencement"
S4/E21

As Zoey's graduation from Georgetown approaches, the President and national security team are alarmed over the disappearance of a group of suspected terrorists. Charlie remembers a promise he and Zoey made while dating, and plans a graduation gift. Danny Concannon has completed his investigation and is about to reveal in print that the Bartlet Administration was behind Shareef's assassination. Partying at a club after commencement, Zoey Bartlet is kidnapped.

1. The missing terrorists are part of what group?
2. How many terrorists disappeared?
3. The gift Charlie wants to give Zoey for graduation is buried in the National Arborteum. What is it?
4. Toby takes Andy to the home of a mutual friend that she has always admired. Why?
5. What happens unexpectedly at the house?
6. Josh finds that being in the National Arboretum at night calls an exotic locale to mind. What is it?
7. Where is the President's commencement speech?
8. When they are speaking privately, Amy asks Donna a very personal question. What does she ask?
9. Jean-Paul spikes Zoey's drink. What with?
10. A Secret Service agent is killed during Zoey's kidnapping. What was her name?

"25"
S4/E22

Grief-stricken by Zoey's kidnapping and uncertain of his own decision-making clarity, President Bartlet invokes the 25th Amendment to surrender his presidential authority until that crisis is past. Since Vice President Hoynes has resigned, the line of succession points to the Speaker of the House. Toby, now a parent of twins, wonders what kind of father he will be.

1. What did Toby and Andy name their newborn son?
2. Who is he named after?
3. In a private moment, Toby confesses something to Leo. What is it?
4. What does Abbey Bartlet start to do that she absolutely shouldn't?
5. In the midst of planning retaliatory strikes on Qumar in the wake of Zoey's kidnapping, an additional spontaneous crisis occurs in the Situation Room. What is it?
6. President Bartlet instructs Leo to quietly assemble the Cabinet. Why?
7. Charlie is sent off to summon someone to the White House. Who?
8. Privately, in the Oval Office, President Bartlet asks new father Toby what he knows now that he didn't know before. What has Toby learned?
9. The Speaker of the House arrives in the Oval Office. What is his name?
10. As Toby has his first private moment with his new babies, he informs his daughter of her name. What is it?

SEASON 4 EPISODE QUIZ ANSWERS

S4E1: "20 Hours in America, Pt. I"
1. Cathy
2. Tyler
3. dry rub
4. Margaret
5. append "I work at the White House" whenever they tell someone their name
6. Anthony Marcus
7. "just rock and roll"
8. Abbey Bartlet's perceived dismissal of the roles of "wife" and "mother"
9. half a grapefruit
10. Peter Lien, 34

S4E1: "20 Hours in America, Pt. II"
1. He puts off shaking the hand of an old man who has shaken the hand of every president since Hoover
2. Mallory
3. "Schmutzy Pants"
4. bitch
5. Charlie
6. buy a house
7. Debbie Fiderer
8. Sam
9. Matt Kelley
10. Notre Dame

S4E2: "College Kids"
1. "It's because it's incredibly hot, and there's no water."
2. 44
3. Jordan Kendall
4. Mike Casper
5. a comment about poisoning the President

6. Sen. Howard Stackhouse
7. In her comment on poisoning him, she referred to him as "President Bartlet", showing respect even when protesting
8. Amy Gardner
9. "The ones who try to say Yes, and the ones who try to say No."
10. Title IX

S4E3: "The Red Mass"
1. 5
2. 2
3. a less structured, more open-ended debate
4. to have only one debate
5. a mass held for the Supreme Court on the Sunday immediately prior to its convening, attended by Congress, the President, and the cabinet
6. that the Red Mass violates the Constitutional separation of Church and State
7. Horton Wilde, the Democrat running for Congress in the California 47th District
8. the 47th (Orange County) is Sam's home district
9. fly things
10. needle exchange (a method of curbing the transmission of HIV among drug users)

S4E4: "Debate Camp"
1. Sam
2. Cornell Rooker
3. He made public statements expressing support for racial profiling by law enforcement
4. to protect her from the radiation from the XW-9 warhead in a silo 93 feet below the Eisenhower putting green
5. Sam
6. CJ learns from a conservative Christian reporter that Rooker is the "first African-American man I've ever heard make sense on racial profiling
7. a prayer list of 365 influential media people

8. Apollo 11
9. that Andy is pregnant with twins
10. Horton Wilde

S4E5: "Game On"
1. "No. No. No. A little bit."
2. she cuts off his necktie
3. that he suspend the Wilde campaign, at the President's request
4. because it has become a national embarrassment
5. Elsie Snuffin
6. Beatrice and Bluto
7. a 10-word answer
8. a belief that ties can be lucky/unlucky
9. 27
10. Uncle Fluffy

S4E6: "Election Night"
1. Josh
2. Toby
3. he wrote a concession speech
4. the wrath of the whatever from high atop the thing
5. go outside, turn around three times, and spit
6. that there is an awareness in Congress that Andy is pregnant, though unmarried
7. an evening cloudburst that keeps people away from the polls
8. he was late
9. takes him to a polling center to vote
10. to switch votes with him, since she accidentally voted for the Republican ticket

S4E7: "Process Stories"
1. unexpectedly, in a live news report from the West Coast, viewed by a crowded West Wing bullpen
2. Sam Donaldson, ABC News
3. issue a statement that he is the father of the babies she is about

to have

4. Christ Whitaker
5. to tell the staff that she thinks Sam should follow through in the run-off campaign in Orange County
6. assuming his posting as NSA Nancy McNally's new aide
7. an ashtray from the submarine USS Greenville, designed to break cleanly into three dull pieces for safety
8. $400
9. Charlie, Sam, Leo, Toby (in that order)
10. "The House of the Rising Sun"

S4E8: "Swiss Diplomacy"

1. A simultaneous heart/lung transplant
2. Japan
3. Karen Kroft
4. Director of the National Parks Service
5. election fraud, for failing to disclose to her pregnancy to her constituents
6. Will has selected someone other than himself to run Sam's campaign, and Sam expected him to do that job
7. one of the family cats
8. the housekeeper
9. Vice President Hoynes
10. President Bartlet

S4E9: "Arctic Radar"

1. Lt. Cmdr. Vickie Hilton
2. for refusing to follow an order that she discontinue an affair she was having with a fellow officer
3. he asks for their resignations
4. that he has been moved from the front row to the fourth row
5. a *Star Trek* pin
6. to ask Lt. Cmdr. Jack Reese if he likes Donna
7. first woman at Miramar; first woman to fly the F-14 Tomcat
8. the UN Secretary General
9. parking tickets

10. "He's one of us"

S4E10: "Holy Night"
1. The Whiffenpoofs
2. Andy's failure to disclose her pregnancy to her constituents
3. Danny Concannon
4. Jules (Julie)
5. The Girl from Ipanema
6. He made women's raincoats
7. He worked for Murder, Inc. (the Jewish mob)
8. He is investigating the disappearance of Abdul Shareef
9. Jean-Paul (Pierre Claude Charpentier Vicomte de Conde)
10. to allow Jean-Paul to accompany her home for the Bartlet family Christmas

S4E11: "Guns Not Butter"
1. Many voters dislike that their tax dollars are going overseas
2. He was at the office all the time.
3. a cow
4. a goat
5. that Jamil Bari doesn't exist; the name is an alias
6. The woman was a private in the army and the letter was about eligibility for food stamps for her family
7. to get the senator to switch her vote on the foreign aid bill
8. a study on the impact of intercessory prayer on medical outcomes
9. Winston Churchill
10. "Democracy is the worst form of government – except for all the others."

S4E12: "The Long Goodbye"
1. Dayton, Ohio
2. Talmidge Cregg
3. a junior high school math teacher
4. Marco Arlens
5. antique watch repair
6. The Mollusk of Lust

7. "The Promise of a Generation"
8. Molly
9. a mohawk
10. his gold pocket watch, a 1931 Hamilton, which Marco has offered to repair

S4E13: "Inauguration, Pt. I"
1. 8
2. a bible for the President's swearing-in
3. he was reassigned for providing the President with a force depletion report behind the back of Secretary Hutchinson
4. that he is beginning to experience dementia
5. The Republic of Equatorial Kundu
6. a genocide is underway; the Arkutu government has begun killing citizens of the Induye tribe
7. "I don't know, sir, but it is."
8. "That was ballsy."
9. 13, according to Donna, who apparently removed a pair from Jack Reese
10. 150

S4E14: "Inauguration: Over There"
1. General Tom Bailey, Supreme Commander, NATO Allied Forces Europe
2. candy, to buy their love
3. a doctrine of humanitarian intervention in other nations
4. a Laurel and Hardy movie including many marching toy soldiers
5. Donna
6. Lt. Cmdr. Jack Reese
7. to make him Deputy Communications Director
8. taking the blame for the critical Washington Post quote, in order to protect Jack
9. Senior Counselor to the President
10. by throwing snowballs at her window

S4E15: "The California 47th"
1. Scott Holcomb
2. "Noel Coward-esque"
3. announce their own tax plan that day, before the President and staff leave for California
4. It includes a tax increase on the richest 1% of Americans, and Orange County – Sam's district – is very, very wealthy
5. Lauren
6. He's a communist
7. that Josh and Toby take it over, because Scott Holcomb is mis-managing it
8. They were harassing Andy Wyatt for being pregnant outside of wedlock
9. He realizes they are withholding announcement of their tax plan in order to avoid harm to his campaign
10. that the audience not let the President leave the stage until he's told them of his own tax plan

S4E16: "Red Haven's on Fire"
1. 3
2. He redirects $12 million from grant funds earmarked for the First Lady's immunization education project
3. Max
4. her nephew
5. Amy Gardner
6. "because it's bloody"
7. sets the table on fire
8. It is the code name of the makeshift training camp where the hostage rescue was rehearsed
9. Cassie
10. 17

S4E17: "Privateers"
1. The Daughters of the American Revolution
2. her qualifying relative was a privateer
3. Clancy Bangart

4. all of her diplomas fall of her office wall; then the doors fall off their hinges
5. Burt Gantz
6. Mike
7. Marion Cotesworth-Haye
8. Marblehead
9. The Francis Scott Key Key
10. she baby-sat for her

S4E198: "Angel Maintenance"
1. Manila
2. recertification of the status of Columbia as a US ally in the war on drugs
3. the President must receive an in-person briefing on the drug situation
4. Will
5. that they can't land because there is fuel spilled all over the runway
6. a "runway incursion"
7. that there have been some friendly fire deaths
8. cleaning up Chesapeake Bay
9. Congressman Mark Richardson, from Toby's own home district
10. Diane Moss

S4E19: "Evidence of Things Not Seen"
1. Joe Quincy
2. The form asks if he has done anything that might embarrass the President; he declines to sign it because, being a Republican, he did not vote for him
3. stand the egg up on its end
4. he's a reserve officer in the Air Force
5. to see who can toss a playing card the farthest
6. 3
7. Cheyenne
8. to interview two Air Force launch crew officers who failed to fire Minuteman missiles at what was supposed to be a North Korean

missile, but turned out to be a meteor
9. that she is going to Paris with Jean-Paul for three months
10. blow it up

S4E20: "Life on Mars"
1. Shyster
2. mayonnaise
3. the Steam Pipe Trunk Distribution Venue, where Ainsley had once worked
4. Stu Winkle
5. Vice President Hoynes
6. Helen Baldwin
7. a pistachio nut
8. the ground
9. White House phone logs
10. a political ad promoting clean air standards

S4E21: "Commencement"
1. The Bahji
2. 5
3. a bottle of champagne
4. He bought her the house in hopes of their remarriage
5. Andy goes into labor
6. A rice paddy in Vietnam
7. written on napkins and stuffed in his pockets
8. if she is in love with Josh
9. ecstasy
10. Molly O'Conner

S4E22: "25"
1. Huck
2. Andy's grandfather
3. that he worries about whether he will love his kids as much as other fathers love theirs
4. She enters the press room, intending to make a direct on-air appeal to Zoey's kidnappers

5. two young men in a small commercial plane wander into air space they shouldn't be in, prompting rapid preparations to shoot them down
6. So that he can inform them that he is about to invoke the 25th Amendment and recuse himself of the presidency
7. a federal judge, to swear in the new president
8. that babies come with hats
9. Glen Allen Walken
10. Molly, after the Secret Service agent who was killed

"7A WF 83429"
S5/E1

With Glenallen Walken now the acting POTUS, Jed Bartlet turns to family matters, as Abbey confronts him with the question of whether her kidnapping was a direct result of Shareef's assassination – which he never discussed with her. Leo advised Walken and is now limited in what he can say to Bartlet; Charlie vigilantly looks out for him. The staff frets over Walken's hawkish tendencies, worried that he will attack Qumar directly. Danny Concannon's embargo of his story revealing the assassination is superseded by the FBI's outing of the five Bahji sleepers, an exclusive on which Danny had been promised by Leo. Meanwhile, the staff scrambles to find a vice president.

1. What does '7A WF 83429' mean?
2. What does the '7A' indicate?
3. The name of the next Speaker of the House is floated by Republicans and discussed by the staff. Who is it?
4. Josh points out that even Republicans consider that nominee a what?
5. President Walken has a constant companion. What is this companion's name?
6. What is CJ's response to Walken's decision to break the news about Shareef before the Washington Post publishes Danny's story?
7. Watching Walken address the press about the Shareef assassination on television with other staffers, Josh describes him how?
8. A reporter asks Walken if he regrets having supported the assassination as Speaker. What is Walken's reply?
9. Leo tells Toby to begin working on two speeches. What are

they?

10. President Bartlet, Abbey, and the rest of the family leave the White House for an event. What is it?

"The Dogs of War"
S5/E2

As the crisis of Zoey Bartlet's kidnapping persists, acting President Walken orders the bombing of Qumar, prompting the kidnappers to issue a demand that American troops be removed from Qumar within 24 hours. Josh grows more anxious that the Republicans will exploit their new power. Toby continues work on the speeches and spends time with his new children.

1. Leo brings a former colleague down from New York to help manage the situation. What is her name?
2. The Secretary of State is in the house. What is his name?
3. Josh returns to his office to find a stranger waiting in it. Who is it?
4. This stranger has a very famous relative. Who?
5. Josh runs into Steve Atwood, from Walken's staff, in a White House men's room. Atwood states that Josh has Republicans all wrong, explaining how they actually feel about what President Bartlet has done. What does he tell Josh?
6. Josh and Ryan have something in common. What?
7. Debbie is a fan of one of the real-world 20th century presidents. Which one?
8. According to Debbie, what did that president call the Oval Office?
9. Apart from the vice presidency, another important federal leader is about to need replacing. Which one?
10. Where is Zoey finally found?

"Jefferson Lives"
S5/E3

With Zoey safe and the Qumar incident receding, President Bartlet and the staff turn their attention to the problem of finding a new vice president. The President's first pick meets with firm opposition from the new speaker, forcing other, lesser candidates into consideration. While Abbey looks after her recovering daughter, Amy minds the store; Josh's new intern Ryan irritates everyone around him.

1. Who is the President's first pick for VP?
2. When Toby expresses his opinion of that candidate to CJ, how does he describe his expression?
3. As Fourth of July celebration arrangements are underway, a bomb scare postpones an event at a VFW hall. What is the event?
4. The President is a Fourth of July buff, and always gives the same talk to those around him on the day. He loves to cite a particular event in US history, referenced in the episode title. What event?
5. Charlie explains to the President that Zoey puts on a brave face for her father. In flashback, we see an example of that; what is Zoey doing in the flashback?
6. The President finally chooses his new VP. Who is it?
7. What state does he represent?
8. What is his nickname?
9. When speaking privately with the VP candidate who finally gets the job, the President notes that he makes an unusual fashion statement. What is it?
10. What is the President's final act of the day, in celebration of the Fourth of July?

"Han"
S5/E4

A visiting North Korean piano prodigy is set to perform at the White House, but could trigger a major perturbation in relations between the two countries. The staff works to get Bob Russell confirmed by the Senate and the House.

1. When meeting President Bartlet, Jai Yung Ahn (the pianist) hands him something. What is it?
2. He writes something on it. What does it say?
3. Donna hosts visitors in the White House. Who are they?
4. The staff has agreed not to use the word *recession* in public, and so they have started substituting it with another word. What word?
5. One Congressman decides to vote against Bob Russell's confirmation as vice president. Which one?
6. CJ informs Charlie that North Korea is the only country left in the world where it is impossible... to do what?
7. Why is Jai's request to defect refused?
8. When President Bartlet approaches Jai to tell him it is best if he does not pursue defection, what is he playing on the piano?
9. Toby lobbies Leo to change his role and responsibilities. How?
10. What does the Korean word *han* mean?

"Constituency of One"
S5/E5

Tempers flare all around the West Wing! Josh's skill in negotiating with Congress is mentioned in a *Washington Post* article, emboldening him to get tough with a senator who is holding up military promotions, leading things a mess. Newly-seated Vice President Russell works to poach a Bartlet staffer for his own; Amy incurs the President's wrath when she oversteps on an issue championed by the First Lady, who is back in New Hampshire looking after Zoey. CJ angers Leo by inserting her own views into the Administration's official line on an EPA report.

1. Which Bartlet staffer is Russell trying to poach?
2. What position does he want to offer that staffer?
3. What's the name of the senator who's holding up the military promotions?
4. What does he want in exchange for releasing the promotions?
5. The *Post* article singing Josh's praises gives him a nickname. What is it?
6. It's a special day for Josh. Why?
7. CJ is getting messages from an old friend. What's his name?
8. What is CJ's problem with the administration's edit of the EPA mining report?
9. Somebody leaves a dead fish on Josh's desk. Who?
10. Josh counters Sen. Carrick's hold on the promotions by embarrassing him in a public statement, outing him for it. What is Carrick's even more devastating response?

"Disaster Relief"
S5/E6

A violent tornado destroys an Oklahoma town, and CJ thinks it's a good idea for President Bartlet to go there and visit the scene – though it sends the White House off the tracks when, overcome with compassion, he stays too long. Josh grows concerned over political errors damaging to the Democrats, and Donna grows concerned over public criticism of Josh.

1. In discussing Josh's predicament with Donna, what term does CJ invoke to describe the anticipated public response?
2. Charlie describes a card game he played with the President until all hours of the morning. The cards were in Latin, and the President claimed they were given to him by whom?
3. What's the Oklahoma governor's last name?
4. Percy Fitzwallace has been replaced as Chairman of the Joint Chiefs. What is his replacement's name?
5. According to Toby, what were the happiest 15 minutes of life?
6. What's the name of the obliterated town the President visits?
7. Who does Leo bring in to take over some of Josh's duties?
8. What was that person's role when working with Leo years earlier?
9. Josh has a dinner scheduled, but the person he was meeting doesn't show. Who appears instead, to help him save face?
10. What do Democrats call their peers who vote with Republicans?

"Separation of Powers"
S5/E7

The Chief Justice of the Supreme Court, already on the President's and Leo's radar for delivering opinions in verse, collapses and is hospitalized. As the President and staff deliberate over what to do about it, Toby recruits someone who once worked for the Chief Justice to make an approach. Meanwhile, Angela Blake takes Josh's place in budget negotiations as Congressional Republicans try to strong-arm the White House. Zoey, recovering from her kidnapping ordeal, prepares to be interviewed on television by a no-holds-barred newswoman.

1. What's the Chief Justice's name?
2. Who does Toby get to approach him?
3. How do they know the Chief Justice?
4. What's the name of the newswoman who will interview Zoey?
5. In the budget negotiations, Angela Blake believes she can get Speaker Haffley and the Republicans to drop their capital gains cut if the White House is willing to drop something that is near and dear to Toby and Josh. What is it?
6. The Republicans abruptly stop negotiating and make a demand: a temporary across-the-board cut on federal spending. At what percent?
7. The Chief Justice meets privately with President Bartlet in the Oval Office. The President says he hopes to consult with the Chief about his possible replacement. What's the first name he suggests?
8. Joe Quincy tells Toby that every year, the very liberal

Chief Justice hires a conservative clerk. Why?

9. Toby talks privately with Joe in his office. He mentions that meeting the Chief Justice is one of those few things in life that doesn't disappoint, and compares him to what?

10. When Speaker Haffley informs President Bartlet in the Roosevelt Room that his caucus and constituents will not settle for less than the across-the-board spending cut, and that if he refuses, the government will be shut down, what is the President's response?

"Shutdown"
S5/E8

The standoff between President Bartlet and House Speaker Haffley has shut down the government, and the President retires to the residence to watch sports as the staff scrambles to figure out what to do next. Leo brings in the big gun, and Josh recommends a bold and very risky solution.

1. Speaker Haffley bumps up the percentage of the across-the-board spending cut. To what?
2. How long did the Roosevelt Room meeting between the President and the Republicans last?
3. Speaker Haffley appears on the cover of what magazine?
4. A perky assistant begins appearing around the West Wing, picking up trash. What is her name?
5. Why did her parents name her that?
6. What does Toby call her?
7. Who does Leo bring in to help resolve the crisis?
8. After weeks in the doghouse, Josh comes back strong. He makes two suggestions for unprecedented gestures, steps the President can take to break the logjam with Haffley. What are they?
9. Once they arrive at the Hill, Haffley puts the President off so he can take time to craft a strategy. Josh makes a third suggestion for an unprecedented gesture on the part of the President. What is it?
10. Amid all the budget chaos, a small and private state dinner is being prepared. Who is it for, and who is preparing it?

"Abu el Banat"
S5/E9

It's Christmas again, and the Bartlet daughters are assembling one-by-one at the White House for a family dinner that never quite comes together. It turns out a member of the family has political ambitions, which causes problems for Leo and Josh. The Attorney General is likewise causing strife, advocating action against an Oregon doctor assisting in suicide. Meanwhile, the President copes with the incarceration of Christian relief workers in Islamic Sudan, as Toby wrestles with Will over having the Vice President address the issue in a speech.

1. What is President Bartlet's son-in-law's name?
2. What is President Bartlet's grandson's name?
3. Why is the DEA's action against the doctor problematic?
4. Which member of the arriving Bartlet family has the political ambition, and what is it?
5. Why is it a problem for Leo and Josh?
6. What activity is Gus excited about?
7. Which Bartlet daughter is last to arrive?
8. President Bartlet's Secret Service codename is Eagle; Zoey's is Bookbag. What is Gus's?
9. What does "Abu el Banat" mean?
10. When a Bedouin meets an Abu el Banat, what does he do for him?

"The Stormy Present"
S5/E10

The death of a former president brings President Bartlet together with two of his predecessors to attend the funeral. Aboard Air Force One, the three discuss their respective administrations and the current situation in the Middle East. Back in Washington, CJ discovers the government is experimenting with mind control, Josh negotiates a battle over the Bill of Rights, and Leo learns that his ex-wife is about to remarry.

1. What's the name of the deceased former president?
2. One of the other former presidents who joins President Bartlet aboard Air Force One is his temporary replacement, Glenallen Walken. Who is the other?
3. Ownership of a copy of the Bill of Rights is in dispute, and two states are fighting over which should have possession of it. Which two states?
4. A scientist appears in CJ's office, talking about government mind-control experiments. What agency is he from?
5. Who tells Leo about his wife's upcoming remarriage?
6. The deceased president had an odd hobby. What was it?
7. Leo is monitoring violent protests occurring in another country. What country?
8. Where specifically are the protestors protesting?
9. The mind-control scientist informs CJ that it is possible to learn a great deal about a person from what feature of their behavior?
10. What Bartlet Administration event did two of the former presidents discuss by phone when it happened?

"The Benign Prerogative"
S5/E11

Toby finishes the State of the Union speech early for once, giving Joey Lucas time to get feedback from a focus group of everyday voters. Abbey lobbies the President to pardon a Native American tribal leader as he is in the process of considering other pardons. A young journalist catches Charlie's eye.

1. What does the episode title refer to?
2. What is the name of the journalist Charlie is attracted to?
3. Where do they meet?
4. Something is very different about Joey Lucas this time. What is it?
5. Toby has a new assistant. Who is it?
6. The staff is discussing a new bill with the President. What kind of bill?
7. Who is assigned to read through the pardon files?
8. Charlie becomes angry with Meeshell. Why?
9. Meeshell and Charlie have an argument in the office outside the Oval. She responds very negatively to something he says, just as the President walks in. What is the nature of this negative response?
10. A young man on Donna's pardon list warrants parole, but the President and staff decide to delay issuing it until the crime bill has passed. What happens as a result?

"Slow News Day"
S5/E12

In a flash of insight, Toby concludes that a moderate Republican senator is intending to retire, and that his retirement represents a brief window of opportunity to move quickly on Social Security reform. He shares his conclusions with President Bartlet before he tells anyone else, and is empowered to quietly make overtures to explore the possibility – but it must remain absolutely quiet, just between the two of them. When it all goes awry, Toby is hard pressed to put the genie back in the bottle. Meanwhile, CJ spars with an aggressive reporter as female staffers gripe about Rina to Josh.

1. What is the Republican senator's name?
2. Why does Toby believe his retirement is an opportunity?
3. In his conversation with Toby, the senator invokes the name of a House Republican who would have been a great advocate of such an effort. What was that congressman's name, and why is he not around to help?
4. Will has a new joke about the Vice President: "Bob Russell is so dull his Secret Service name is _____"?
5. Toby needs some quiet research done. Who does he enlist to do it?
6. A dashing representative from the Argentine embassy appears in CJ's office. What does he want to discuss?
7. Josh figures Toby is up to something and conspires to find out what. How does he go about it?
8. Faced with failing in the Social Security reform effort and embarrassing the administration, what does Toby offer the President?
9. Who comes to Toby's aid and gives the project the missing piece it needs?

10. The Senate Republican and Democrat who are willing to make the deal get one final gesture from the President and his team to seal it. What is it?

"The Warfare of Genghis Khan"
S5/E13

Satellite imagery from over the Indian Ocean disclose a new nuclear player in the world, in the unsettling domain of the Middle East. As President Bartlet and his national security team go to work figuring out who it is, Iran arouses the greatest concern. Meanwhile, Josh has a run-in with NASA, as CJ has a run-in with a feisty talk show host.

1. What's the name of the talk show host who baits CJ?
2. In baiting her, what does he call her?
3. Who does Leo try hard to brief about the nuclear test?
4. CJ has been dodging phone calls. From who?
5. An attractive NASA administrator follows up with Josh after he is dismissive to her group in a White House meeting, describing an inspirational new space initiative, abbreviated "M.O.B." What does it stand for?
6. Josh mentions to Donna that an unmanned spacecraft (that really exists) launched long ago has just left the solar system. Which spacecraft?
7. Who delivers the essential clue to the identity of the new nuclear nation?
8. Which nation is the new nuclear player?
9. What was the clue?
10. As the identity of the new nuclear player is discovered, a bombing mission has been launched against another nation and must be recalled. What nation was about to be bombed?

"An Khe"
S5/E14

An old friend of Leo's is a top executive in the defense industry, and Leo speaks at a banquet in his honor. And when an Air Force Thunderchief is shot down by the North Koreans, Leo finds himself recalling that he and his old friend were shot down in Vietnam, and his friend got him to safety. As the President sends Navy SEALs to recover the crew of the Thunderchief, CJ goes on the Taylor Reid Show to spar with the belligerent host, and Ryan embarrasses Josh in front of the President by out-thinking him.

1. What is Leo's old friend's name?
2. The President is balking at facilitating a traditional presidential ritual. What is it?
3. Where is the crew of the downed plane?
4. Someone from CJ's past finally makes an in-person appearance in the West Wing. Who?
5. Republican Congressman Wendt is proposing an amendment to the tax code that draws Josh's ire. What is it?
6. Abbey has decided to begin doing something that might be controversial. What is it?
7. In an attempt to get under CJ's skin during their interview, Taylor Reid calls global warming by two derogatory names. What are they?
8. What does Leo want to do for his old friend that Josh and Toby – and the President, for that matter - won't let him do?
9. Leo's friend won't let him do it, either. Why not?
10. When President Bartlet visits Leo in his office later, there is music playing; it is a real-world rock group. Who is it, and what is the song?

"Full Disclosure"
S5/E15

John Hoynes is back, teasing his intentions to run for president in the next election – about which CJ is blindsided, live on Taylor Reid's talk show. Toby haggles with trade union reps as Josh talks school vouchers with DC's mayor and intern Ryan shows Josh up yet again in a meeting with a congressman over military base closings.

1. What does Taylor Reid hit CJ with concerning former Vice President John Hoynes?
2. Hoynes has written a book that is about to be released as part of a presidential run. What is its title?
3. CJ reaches out to a *New York Times* reporter. Who?
4. The trade union reps Toby meets with are from what organization?
5. When the mayor of Washington, DC arrives to meet with the President to discuss school vouchers, he surprises him. How?
6. Charlie proceeds to surprise the President even more. How?
7. The trade reps that a certain Chinese product is "killing us", as they flood Wal-Marts everywhere with it. What product?
8. CJ wants the *New York Times* reporter to give her advance notice of the specific Hoynes quotes in his upcoming article. How does he accommodate her?
9. What disclosure about CJ's past encounters with Hoynes is made?
10. Exhausted, CJ ends her day in her office, talking to someone – or rather, just listening to them – on the phone. Who?

"Eppur Si Muove"
S5/E16

President Bartlet grows angry when a conservative congresswoman tries to shut down an NIH research project, to which his daughter Ellie is contributing. Toby and Rina investigate the leak that led to Ellie's outing in the press, as Josh fights to keep an old friend on track for a federal judge appointment and Abbey and CJ meet the Muppets.

1. What is the lab to which Ellie belongs researching?
2. Why is the study controversial?
3. What is Ellie's professional rank now?
4. Where is the lab in which she's working located?
5. What is being researched is the cause of cervical cancer. In the episode, it's mentioned that someone died of cervical cancer. Why?
6. What's the name of the conservative congresswoman who is generating grief over the research?
7. What does "Eppur Si Muove" mean, and what is its significance?
8. Who was ultimately behind the leak?
9. Who figures out who that person was and confronts them?
10. Which Muppet was also on *Sesame Street*?

"The Supremes"
S5/E17

A SCOTUS justice has died, and it falls to the President to nominate a successor - though getting someone truly effective past the Senate presents a challenge. The staff interview several good candidates, but it isn't until Donna receives a gift from home that Josh is inspired to present the President with a game-changing solution.

1. What's the name of the deceased justice?
2. Toby and Josh meet with a potential nominee who immediately impresses Josh. What is her name?
3. Speaking privately to Toby, Josh gushes, "I love her mind!" What else does he love about her?
4. Josh and Toby assume the Senate will not confirm her, based on a controversial ruling she once made. What was it?
5. Even if she gets past that hurdle, there's a private matter from her past which, if discovered, would ensure that she isn't confirmed. What is it?
6. A suitable moderate gets as far as a face-to-face meeting with President Bartlet. What is his name?
7. Josh figures out a way, not only to get the controversial judge they really want, but to put her in the ailing Chief Justice Ashland's seat. What is it?
8. Where does he get the idea?
9. What's the name of the ultra-conservative judge the Republican's pick?
10. The new Chief Justice signs an autograph that will someday be gifted to Toby's infant daughter Molly. What does she sign?

"Access"
S5/E18

A documentary on White House press secretaries includes CJ, and a television crew follows her around, just as a national crisis erupts, once again testing her ability to juggle the press and security concerns. While this is going on, President Bartlet is preparing to meet the pope.

1. Who is producing the documentary?
2. Behind the scenes, the White House is working with the FBI on a domestic hostage situation. Where is the hostage situation happening?
3. A similar situation occurred very early in the first term of the Bartlet Administration. Where was the incident in that earlier case?
4. In the midst of it all, CJ receives a private phone call in her office. From who?
5. A ritual among White House press secretaries is the passing of a growing patch of notes of advice from predecessors. In what are these notes contained?
6. A familiar face keeps CJ informed of the FBI's rescue efforts. Who is it?
7. While waiting for the outcome of the hostage situation, President Bartlet takes the time to meet with a group. What group?
8. The President joins the Ugandan Health Minister in meeting with the press – to discuss what?
9. Leo is seen meeting with a federal official near the end of the episode. Who?
10. After such a tumultuous series of events, who tells CJ she had a good day?

"Talking Points"
S5/E19

As the President is preparing to travel to Europe for an international trade summit, Josh is surprised to learn that he is changing his stance on letting US jobs go overseas. He is confronted by a group of high-tech workers who are in just such a position, demanding to know what the White House is going to do about it. CJ learns that new FCC rules expand the number of TV stations that multimedia companies can own – a monopoly-strengthening policy. Donna is growing dissatisfied with her role, and a new face appears in the West Wing.

1. Where is the international trade summit to be held?
2. The White House is surrounded. By what?
3. One nation in particular has had problems with the trade agreement, and Josh is surprised when he learns its concerns have been abated. What nation is it?
4. A negative consequence of the trade agreement is that a great many US jobs will be moved to that country. What kind of jobs?
5. How many Americans will lose those jobs?
6. CJ is incensed by the FCC ruling. Why?
7. A small group of displaced computer programmers tell Josh their name for the government transition assistance he offers as consolation. What is it?
8. A new character is introduced in this episode. Who is it?
9. What is their White House role?
10. Annoyed by the press corps' lack of interest in the FCC story, CJ orders the number of seats in the press room reduced to the number of big media corporations. How many seats are left?

"No Exit"
S5/E20

The White House is on lock-down once again – only this time, it's due to a possible contagion. The President and staff are not just sequestered in the building; they are quarantined wherever they happen to be. Lots of cathartic soul-searching and anger-venting ensues, as Toby is trapped with Will, Donna is stuck with CJ, Josh gets to know the new NSA deputy, and the President settles in with Charlie and Debbie.

1. In the Presidential limousine, Debbie has the sniffles. Why?
2. Where have they just been?
3. Josh is miffed about the President's monologue at the dinner. Why?
4. Where are Toby and Will, and what do they argue about?
5. Where are Josh and Kate Harper, and what do they talk about?
6. Where are CJ and Donna, and what do they talk about?
7. Donna is about to leave the country. Where is she going, and why?
8. Abbey sits out the lockdown with Leo. Where are they and what do they talk about?
9. As Charlie is speaking privately with Agent Butterfield about the source of the contamination, Debbie comments to the President, "He won't forgive himself." Why not?
10. In the decontamination area with Charlie and the President, Debbie notes that although many games such as Boggle and Risk have been stocked, there is one important omission: what is it?

"Gaza"
S5/E21

On a fact-finding mission to the Gaza Strip, a Congressional delegation including Donna, Toby's ex-wife Andrea Wyatt, and former Joint Chiefs Chairman Fitzwallace are attacked. As President Bartlet considers possible military responses, flashbacks fill in the days before the attack.

1. Donna begins keeping company with an Irish photojournalist who shows the real behind-the-scenes Gaza. What is his name?
2. One of the delegation's vehicles is blown up, with several people inside. Who are they?
3. Who lives, and who dies?
4. Where is Donna flown for treatment?
5. As the White House Deputy Chief of Staff, Josh has a diplomatic rank equal to what other federal official?
6. Who goes with the President to see the widow of one of those who was killed in the bombing?
7. The top Palestinian official speaks to President Bartlet on the phone, disavowing the incident in Gaza. What is his name?
8. What injuries did Donna suffer?
9. Admiral Fitzwallace was mentor to someone else in the administration. Who?
10. When Charlie's mother was killed in the line of duty, someone called Charlie to offer condolences. Who?

"Memorial Day"
S5/E22

In the aftermath of the Gaza bombing, President Bartlet is pressed by the Speaker, Congress, and even Leo to strike back. Resisting the pressure, he plans a peace summit instead. Josh, who has traveled to Germany to be at Donna's side, is surprised to be covertly contacted by a foreign agent. In this tense atmosphere, Toby and Charlie prep the President, who cannot throw, for a ceremonial first pitch at an upcoming Memorial Day baseball game.

1. The episode opens with word of another attack. Who attacks whom?
2. In a flashback to Bartlet's first days as President-elect, he is visited and briefed by Leo and a former military colleague of Leo's, seen in an earlier episode. Who?
3. The briefing they give Gov. Bartlet concerns a peacekeeping mission in what nation?
4. Someone else appears at the German hospital to visit Donna. Who?
5. Between somber international phone calls, Toby and Charlie spirit the President away to don a bullet-proof vest and practice his throwing. Where does this happen?
6. One of the President's advisors pushes back against immediate retaliatory action. Which one?
7. How is Josh contacted by the covert foreign agent?
8. Kate Harper gives Josh instructions, after he informs the White House about the contact by the foreign agent. What does she ask him to do?
9. Who sent the foreign agent who meets secretly with Josh?
10. A peace summit at Camp David is arranged. A Middle Eastern leader publicly accepts an invitation, though they weren't invited. Who?

SEASON 5 EPISODE QUIZ ANSWERS

S5E1: "7A WF 83429"
1. It's the name of the FBI file on Zoey's kidnapping
2. a Missing Persons case
3. Washington Rep. Jeff Haffley
4. a fascist
5. Bess, his dog
6. She privately urges Danny to publish it immediately
7. "presidential"
8. "My only regret is that we only got to kill the bastard once."
9. a speech for President Bartlet to present if Zoey is recovered alive, another for if she isn't
10. a private Mass at St. Joseph's

S5E2: "The Dogs of War"
1. Angela Blake
2. Lewis Berryhill
3. Ryan Pierce, his new unwanted intern
4. Franklin Pierce, the 14th President of the US
5. Republicans "are in awe of Bartlet"
6. They both went to Harvard
7. Harry Truman
8. "The crown jewel of the American penal system"
9. The Chairman of the Joint Chiefs; Admiral Fitzwallace has announced his intention to retire
10. in a barn near Calverton, Virginia

S5E3: "Jefferson Lives"
1. Secretary of State Lewis Berryhill
2. "This is my over-the-moon face"
3. A swearing-in ceremony for new immigrating citizens
4. The deaths of John Adams and Thomas Jefferson on the same day, July 4, 1826 (the 50th anniversary of the Declaration of Independence) - "Jefferson lives" were John Adams' last words

5. a very young Zoey is riding a huge horse
6. Rep. Robert (Bob) Russell
7. Colorado
8. "Bingo Bob"
9. He wears cowboy boots
10. He leads the new immigrants in their oath of citizenship

S5E4: "Han"
1. a CD
2. "I wish to defect"
3. her Aunt Barbara and Uncle Ted from Wisconsin
4. *bagel*
5. Congressman Theo, Democrat from Rhode Island
6. access the Internet
7. It will disrupt secret talks in progress with North Korea on their nuclear armament program
8. Chopin
9. He wants to take over shaping the administration's long-term message, and have Will take over his day-to-day responsibilities
10. a sadness so deep, no tears will come; and yet still, there's hope

S5E5: "Constituency of One"
1. Will
2. to be his chief strategist
3. Chris Carrick of Idaho
4. a contract with the Pentagon to have a questionable new missile launcher built in his state
5. "The 101st Senator"
6. It's his birthday
7. Ben
8. that the administration edited it at all, and that it touts "clean coal", which she thinks is dishonest
9. Amy
10. he leaves the Democratic Party and joins the Republican Party

S5E6: "Disaster Relief"
1. schadenfreude
2. Frank Sinatra
3. Wade
4. Gen. Nicholas Alexander
5. Imagining what he would name a boat, if he bought it
6. Maysville
7. Angela Blake
8. She was his second-in-command when he was Secretary of Labor
9. Ryan Pierce
10. Blue Dogs

S5E7: "Separation of Powers"
1. Roy Ashland
2. Joe Quincy
3. He once clerked for Ashland
4. Diane Mathers
5. deductible tuition
6. 1%
7. Oliver Wendall Holmes
8. to argue with
9. The Grand Canyon
10. "Then shut it down."

S5E8: "Shutdown"
1. 3%
2. 6 minutes
3. *Time*
4. Rina (Marina)
5. She was born on a boat
6. "a walking lawsuit"
7. Abbey, who has been in New Hampshire looking after Zoey
8. that the President go to the Hill to meet with Haffley; and that he walk there, in full view of the world
9. that they get up and leave, as the media's cameras roll

10. The British Prime Minister and his wife; Abbey, cooking 'Coronation chicken' - the Queen's own recipe

S5E9: "Abu el Banat"
1. Doug Weston
2. Gus
3. Physician-assisted suicide is legal in Oregon
4. Doug; he wants to run for Congress from New Hampshire
5. The Democratic Party doesn't want him
6. He and his grandfather are going to perform the ceremonial lighting of the Christmas tree on the White House grounds
7. Ellie
8. Tonka
9. "father of daughters"
10. offers him tea

S5E10: "The Stormy Present"
1. Owen Lassiter
2. D. Wire Newman
3. North Carolina and Connecticut
4. DARPA (Defense Advanced Research Projects Agency)
5. Mallory, his daughter
6. traveling to countries where US soldiers had been killed and collecting soil samples
7. Saudi Arabia
8. In Riyadh, the capitol, where they have surrounded an American oil facility
9. their gait
10. President Lassiter called President Newman when Bartlet's multiple sclerosis was announced

S5E11: "The Benign Prerogative"
1. The "benign prerogative" refers to the President's power to pardon
2. Meeshell
3. at a party hosted by Angela Blake

4. She is very pregnant
5. Rina, whom he met during the shutdown
6. a crime bill
7. Donna
8. She kept from him that she has been assigned to join the White House press corps, as he had been sharing tidbits of information with her
9. She slaps him
10. He takes his own life

S5E12: "Slow News Day"
1. Steve Gaines
2. If Gaines is not running for reelection, he has nothing to lose by going all in on Social Security reform
3. Jim Carney; Josh and Toby wrote an attack ad that got him voted out
4. "Bob Russell"
5. Rina
6. cabbage
7. He sends Donna in to cozy up to Rina and get her to tell her what she's working on
8. his resignation
9. Josh
10. They agree not to take credit for any of it

S5E13: "The Warfare of Genghis Khan"
1. Taylor Reid
2. "Chicken of the Week"
3. Vice President Russell
4. her old flame Ben
5. Mars or Bust
6. Voyager I
7. Vice President Russell
8. Israel
9. that Israel now has nuclear submarines
10. Iran

S5E14: "An Khe"

1. Ken O'Neal
2. sitting for an official portrait
3. hiding in the North Korean wilderness
4. Ben
5. a subsidy for stay-at-home moms
6. volunteering at a Washington free clinic, when she has given up her medical license
7. "liberal fantasy" and "voodoo environmentalism"
8. He wants to testify on O'Neal's behalf before a Congressional committee
9. Ken O'Neal is, in fact, guilty of circumventing DoD procurement protocols
10. Crosby, Stills & Nash, singing "My Country, 'Tis of Thee"

S5E15: "Full Disclosure"

1. a Sunday *Times* magazine interview in which Hoynes claims that the President tried to instigate a cover-up of Hoynes' indiscretions
2. *Full Disclosure*
3. Greg Brock
4. the AFL-CIO
5. by expressing openness to a tuition voucher program, which Democrats traditionally eschew
6. that he wishes such a voucher program had been in place when he was in high school
7. bras
8. by dropping a computer disk containing a copy of the story on the floor of her office
9. that he cheated on his wife with her
10. Ben

S5E16: "Eppur Si Muove"

1. HPV
2. The study includes Puerto Rican sex workers as subjects
3. post-doctoral fellow
4. Johns Hopkins, her alma mater

5. Debbie Fiderer's sister
6. Barbara Layton
7. "And yet it moves" - what Galileo is alleged to have said when told by the Catholic Church that his theory about the Earth rotating around the sun was heresy
8. Vice President Russell
9. Will
10. Kermit the Frog

S5E17: "The Supremes"
1. Owen Brady
2. Evelyn Baker Lang
3. her shoes
4. She struck down a parental consent law
5. While in law school, she had an abortion
6. E(lijah) Bradford Shelton
7. Get Chief Justice Ashland to stand down, which he would do for another "liberal lion", and offer the Republicans their pick of anyone they like for Brady's seat
8. From a cookie tin with a picture of Donna's parents' cats on it; they could not agree on one cat, so they each got a cat
9. Christopher Mulready
10. a copy of the 14th amendment

S5E18: "Access"
1. PBS
2. Shaw Island, Washington
3. Casey Creek, Kentucky
4. her father
5. a flak jacket
6. Agent Mike Casper
7. a Boy Scout troop
8. AIDS in Africa
9. the Director of the FBI
10. Leo

S5E19: "Talking Points"

1. Brussels
2. 200 tractors
3. India
4. computer programming jobs
5. 17,000
6. It will place more local TV stations under the control of a small handful of big multimedia owners, narrowing the diversity of the news
7. burial insurance
8. Cmdr. Kate Harper
9. Deputy NSC Director
10. 7

S5E20: "No Exit"

1. allergies; high pollen count
2. The annual White House Correspondents Dinner
3. Cmdr. Harper cut a joke he wrote from the President's monologue
4. Will's old office next to Toby's; Toby is angry over Will's defection
5. Josh's office; the lockdown itself, and why she really cut his joke
6. CJ's office; that Josh should have advanced Donna's career a long time ago, but keeps her in place out of convenience
7. Gaza, along with Fitzwallace and a Congressional delegation
8. In the residence; Leo is not crazy about the First Lady's clinical volunteer work
9. He believes he is inadvertently responsible for the presence of the airborne contaminant and possibly endangering the President
10. a deck of playing cards

S5E21: "Gaza"

1. Colin Ayres
2. Donna, Admiral Fitzwallace, Congressmen Korb and DeSantos, and the driver
3. Admiral Fitzwallace and the two congressmen are killed; Donna survives, but is critically injured
4. Landstuhl Medical Center, near Ramstein Air Base, Germany

5. a three-star general
6. Kate Harper
7. Chairman (Nizar) Farad
8. a collapsed lung and a broken thigh bone
9. Kate Harper
10. her captain

S5E22: "Memorial Day"
1. Israel makes a missile strike on Gaza City
2. USAF Lt. Gen. Alan Adamle
3. The Philippines
4. Colin Ayres
5. in a hallway in the residence that is filled with breakable objects
6. Kate Harper
7. in a coded note received with flowers sent to Donna's hospital room
8. have a clandestine meeting with the agent
9. the Palestinian Prime Minister (Mukarat)
10. Palestinian Chairman Farad

"NSF Thurmont"
S6/E1

President Bartlet and his team consider a summit to negotiate a peaceful settlement to the Israeli/Palestinian conflict. Leo, in open disagreement with the President about his approach to the problem, is left behind at the White House. Over in Germany, Donna is rushed back into surgery.

1. The episode opens with a funeral. For whom?
2. Colin Ayres, the photographer who became involved with Donna, is talking with John in the hospital in Germany. Where is Colin from?
3. Why does Donna need additional surgery?
4. Donna sees Josh for a brief moment just before she is taken into surgery. She cannot speak, so she writes him a note. What does it say?
5. She writes a second note, just before they take her away. What does it say?
6. The President and Leo are at odds. How so?
7. A Republican delegation is preparing to take an action to force the President to take military action. What is it?
8. When the President and Abbey talk privately later on, they agree on one of the President's personal traits. What is it?
9. What is the name of the Israeli prime minister?
10. What does NSF Thurmont refer to?

"The Birnam Wood"
S6/E2

President Bartlet and the staff meet with the Israeli Prime Minister and the Palestinian Chairman at Camp David, amid doubts from all sides that the talks will go anywhere. Tensions rise, and tragedy strikes.

1. The FBI delivers conclusive evidence of who was responsible for the Gaza attack. What is the President's retaliatory response?
2. As the President, staff, and the Israeli and Palestinian delegations begin discussions, what central topic is avoided?
3. Back at the White House, CJ is cheered by a welcome appearance. Of whom?
4. President Bartlet, Charlie, Will, Josh, and Toby discuss the negotiations while squeezing in a little recreation. What kind?
5. Arriving at Camp David, Abbey notices a conspicuous absence and asks her husband about it. Who does she ask about?
6. There is much discussion of "Right of Return". What does that refer to?
7. The President and First Lady are invited to a Jewish ritual by the Israelis. What is it?
8. While that ritual is taking place, what are the Palestinians doing?
9. Frustrated over the negotiations, Palestinian Chairman Farad opens up to a member of the Bartlet team. Who?
10. A terrible event ends the episode, preceded by an unthinkable one. What are they?

"Third-Day Story"
S6/E3

As the President prepares to sign the peace accord, he asks Josh and Toby to secure support in the House, as CJ seeks confirmation of international support. In the West Wing, Charlie is on the edge of graduation but is stalling, as Donna arrives, wheelchair-bound, to resume her job.

1. What college requirement is Charlie putting off?
2. Why is he putting it off?
3. Leo collapsed, alone, when he had a heart attack; where was he found?
4. The Republican Leadership attempts to exploit the White House's need for support on the accord by holding out for 60 Democratic votes. On what?
5. CJ insists that Josh lay off a bad habit for a week. What bad habit?
6. CJ says that if he succeeds, she will reward him. How?
7. With Leo out, there are communication problems among the senior staff. Josh and Toby, for instance, agree to contradictory conditions on a feature of the tax cut. What feature?
8. A reporter from the press room pushes CJ hard on an answer to a particular question. What is it?
9. Who is the reporter?
10. Realizing that the White House staff needs a chief, President Bartlet consults a weak, bedridden Leo on who it should be. He approaches that staffer, asking them to do the same thing he asked of Leo when he first offered him the job. Who, and what?

"Liftoff"
S6/E4

New-to-the-job CJ, now White House Chief of Staff, deals with some hazing, some internal administration push-back, and some out-of-the-blue challenges. Josh, working on the tax cut, meets with a congressman who will reshape both their futures.

1. Which staffers haze CJ?
2. How do they haze her?
3. CJ meets with a Georgian diplomat, who offers her something so unbelievable that she assumes it's another hazing. What does he offer her?
4. To deal with the Georgian situation, CJ assembles an interagency team. What are such teams called?
5. A member of the team tries to go around CJ in dealing with what the Georgians are offering. Who?
6. Two future career options appear on Josh's radar, but he isn't interested. What are they?
7. Surprised that one congressman in particular won't be running for re-election, Josh goes to meet with him on Capitol Hill. What is this congressman's name?
8. What state does he represent?
9. What issue does this congressman champion?
10. A new face appears in the West Wing, initially to help Toby and Donna find a new Press Secretary. Who is it?

"The Hubbert Peak"
S6/E5

Josh plays the role of hip modern consumer, checking out a pricey and politically dicey new acquisition. He then meets with some belligerent private sector folks. CJ visits Leo to check on how he's doing. Annabeth takes on the White House Press Corps. Charlie gets a new job.

1. What is it that Josh checks out?
2. Why is it politically dicey?
3. What happens when he investigates this purchase?
4. The incident is deeply ironic, given Josh's original intent. What was that?
5. What does the title refer to?
6. In this fuel standards-themed episode, Josh meets with a group from the private sector. Who are they?
7. CJ visits Leo to see how he's doing. Leo is more interested in how the President is doing. What does he instruct CJ to do?
8. Faced with leaving his job at the President's side due to his graduation, Charlie hands out his resume to several senior staffers. What does he instruct them to do with it?
9. Charlie does, in fact, wind up taking a new job. What is it?
10. Josh drops an amusing reference to a popular movie from the Eighties. What is the reference and what is the movie?

"The Dover Test"
S6/E6

The first casualties from the peacekeeping mission in the Gaza occur, creating negative sentiment in the US; CJ, Toby and Annabeth confer on how best to deal with it. Josh is confounded by Congressman Santos's handling of the Patients Bill of Rights; Leo gets schooled by his nurse.

1. There's a code phrase the senior staff uses to covertly communicate to one another that something important has happened. What is the code phrase?
2. Matt Santos comes to the White House to give Josh a heads up. About what?
3. Will shows up later, angry with Josh. About what?
4. As is customary, the President has Debbie put through a call to the parents of the American soldier who was among those killed. What unexpectedly happens?
5. What is the Dover Test?
6. Toby is accosted by White House reporters in his briefing on the Gaza casualties. What about?
7. Taking a walk through the corridors of the hotel where he has been living, Leo runs into an old business associate. In the midst of their upbeat conversation, Leo suffers sudden embarrassment. Over what?
8. Tracking down Santos to berate him over the bipartisan compromise on the Patient's Bill of Rights, Josh and Will are publicly berated by the congressman. He chastises them for a compromise of their own. What is it?
9. Annabeth pitches an idea for CJ about dealing with the blowback over the Gaza casualties. What is it?
10. Santos has been playing Josh with his handling of the bill. How?

"A Change is Gonna Come"
S6/E7

A Taiwanese delegation visits the White House just as the President is preparing for a state visit to China, leading to a diplomatic uproar. Now that Charlie is working for CJ, the President gets a new body man. John Hoynes, now running for president, begins recruiting.

1. The Taiwanese delegation presents the President with a gift, leading to the uproar. What is it?
2. Why is it a problem?
3. What's the name of the President's new body man?
4. Hoynes wrote a book as a prelude to his campaign. He signs a copy that he gives to Josh. What does it say?
5. Where is the gift presented to the President by the Taiwanese delegation?
6. Charlie searches for the controversial gift; the trail leads to the Gifts Unit, now headed by the former head of the White House Visitors Office. Who is this?
7. A photo is taken in the Oval Office, involving the letter that temporarily removed him from power. Who is there to receive the letter?
8. Someone horns in on the photo op, drawing a private reprimand from the President. Who?
9. There is a presumption that the President was being cagey when he accepted the controversial flag. Abbey discovers the real reason: what is it?
10. A very famous real-world pop star performs at the White House National Medal for the Arts reception. Who is it?

"In the Room"
S6/E8

As the President prepares to fly to China, two famous entertainers visit the White House to help celebrate a special occasion, causing a tremendous controversy. As Air Force One gets underway, the President suffers a major MS episode. Back at home, Josh is approached with an offer to be Bob Russell's campaign manager.

1. What's the special occasion at the White House?
2. Who are the famous entertainers?
3. What do they do that's controversial?
4. Which senior staffer goes nuts over their refusal to cooperate, and what does he demand of them?
5. Air Force One has a not-so-coincidental someone on board who can help the President through the episode. Who?
6. The President has told Josh who he has in mind to take over as UN Ambassador. Who is it?
7. When Josh meets with them to offer them the job, what are they doing?
8. What job do they want instead?
9. Someone announces they will not run for the Democratic nomination for president. Who?
10. The President is paralyzed, but insists on meeting with the press corps aboard Air Force One. How does he do this?

"Impact Winter"
S6/E9

The President and his entourage, now in China, proceed with the summit, despite his indisposition from his MS episode. Appropriately, an asteroid is hurtling toward the earth. Donna leaves the White House.

1. There is an argument over who will announce the President's MS episode to the press. Who ends up doing it?
2. The announcer tells the press where they were when they heard the news about the President. Where was that?
3. The announcer makes a second announcement after sharing the news about the President – that an official event will occur. What event?
4. Who meets Air Force One when it lands in China?
5. NASA notifies the White House about the asteroid. How long until it will arrive?
6. Donna keeps trying to book time with Josh for a private conversation. About what?
7. What topics are the President's top priorities in his discussions with the Chinese?
8. What is the name of Donna's replacement?
9. Josh instructs his new assistant to book a plane flight for him. Where to?
10. Who does he see when he gets there?

"Faith-Based Initiative"
S6/E10

Donna gets a new job as CJ copes with media speculation about her sexual orientation. Already encumbered by the effects of MS, the President has to deal with a senator who is holding up his budget over a pet issue. Josh's pick for the next president agrees to run, on one condition.

1. What is Donna's new job?
2. What's the name of the senator who is holding up the budget?
3. What does he want in exchange for his cooperation?
4. Which administration official refuses to help the President get the votes he needs on the budget?
5. Toby learns that someone was behind the scenes, getting Wilkinson to hold up the budget. Who?
6. Who is Josh's pick for the next president?
7. What is that person's condition for running?
8. What is the Vice President's nephew's name?
9. In a burst of word salad over the press's speculation about her sexual orientation, CJ refers to her potential reputation as "The most..." What?
10. What is CJ's answer to the press, regarding her sexual orientation?

"Opposition Research"
S6/E11

Josh and Matt Santos head for New Hampshire to set up headquarters for their campaign and begin tussling over what the campaign is going to be. Donna begins working with Will on the Russell campaign, and must come to terms with no longer working for Josh.

1. Josh wants Santos to be thinking "retail politics" in these early days of the campaign, rather than big-picture policy. What does Santos want to talk about?
2. A Bartlet daughter appears at Santos campaign headquarters. Which one?
3. A familiar White House reporter takes Josh aside to talk. Which one?
4. What does the reporter tell Josh?
5. Someone arrives to help the Santos campaign with research. Who?
6. The reporter later takes Josh aside to let him know that the press isn't actually covering Santos; they're covering someone else. Who?
7. Josh suggests a common campaign practice that they may wish to undertake, though they may not need it; Santos forbids it. What is that practice?
8. Santos assumes that the researcher is digging up information on the opposition. Josh tells him that isn't the case; who is the researcher researching?
9. The Bartlet daughter gives Josh something. What?
10. Who does Josh accuse of leaking information on Santos to the Associated Press?

"365 Days"
S6/E12

Leo returns to the White House as an advisor, and hopes to meet with senior staff to discuss the Bartlet Administration's final year. A number of crises erupt, however, disrupting his efforts; in a matter of minutes, each staffer is called away.

1. Where does Leo try to conduct his 365 Days meeting?
2. CJ is called away from the meeting; what for?
3. Kate Harper is pulled away from the meeting; what for?
4. Charlie and Annabeth leave to discuss something. What?
5. Toby is pulled away from the meeting; what for?
6. Annabeth meets with the First Lady to discuss her appearance at an upcoming event. What event?
7. CJ goes to the Oval Office to see the President, but Debbie informs her he's not there. Where is he?
8. The Bolivians who have kidnapped the US contractors say they will release them when a demand is met. What demand?
9. Annabeth neglects to inform the First Lady about a particular aspect of the event at which she will appear. It involves an awkward news clip from the event. What is it?
10. The Governor of South Dakota calls CJ about Mount Rushmore. What has happened at Mount Rushmore?

.

"King Corn"
S6/E13

It's Iowa Caucus time, and three presidential candidates – Vice President Russell, Matt Santos on the Democratic side, Arnold Vinick on the Republican side – all must give an address at the Iowa Corn Growers' Expo, where they must speak to the issue of ethanol. Josh wrestles with how he can possibly coach Santos on how to campaign effectively.

1. Everyone shown to wake in this episode has their alarm set for the same time. What time is that?
2. There's a common political term for supporting ethanol. What is it?
3. Which of the three candidates addressing the corn growers doesn't advocate for ethanol?
4. With seeming determination to never take Josh's advice, Santos is seen talking in a diner about an issue other than ethanol. What issue?
5. What is Santos's wife's name?
6. What's the name of Vinick's campaign manager?
7. What's the name of the Vinick campaign's communication manager?
8. What is the name of Santos's congressional aide who serves on his campaign?
9. Someone is Santos's entourage is displeased with Josh nudging Santos away from his priorities. Who?
10. Santos and Vinick have a private conversation. Where are they when this happens?

"The Wake Up Call"
S6/E14

A British passenger plane is shot down over the Middle East, causing the British government to rush toward retaliation as President Bartlet calls in Lord John Marbury for advice on how to intervene. CJ wrestles with the President's new sleep requirements, and Toby hosts a law professor who is on hand to help a newly-emerging democracy to write its own constitution.

1. Who notifies CJ about the downed British plane?
2. What is the name of the law professor who visits the White House?
3. What country is taking up democracy and needing its own constitution?
4. It's a holiday. Which one?
5. A beauty pageant winner also visits the White House. What country is she from?
6. What does the British prime minister want to do in retaliation for the downing of the plane?
7. President Bartlet was sleep-deprived from being woken early by CJ to deal with the crisis, but he was more deprived still; why?
8. Who is displeased with CJ for waking the President early?
9. The Iranians report that shooting down the British airliner was unintentional, a mistake. How did it happen?
10. What is the British prime minister's name?

"Freedonia"
S6/E15

The critical New Hampshire primary is coming up fast, and Josh is desperate to keep Santos competitive. A local paper is hosting a debate between Russell and Hoynes, and Josh conspires to get Santos into the debate. In the meantime, Amy Gardner reappears.

1. What is the significance of the name 'Freedonia'?
2. Why does Amy Gardner reappear?
3. Josh persuades Russell to ask the editor of the newspaper to open the debate to all candidates. Why does Russell go along?
4. Santos is permitted to go to Russell's meeting with the editor, but Josh advises him to stay quiet. He doesn't; he speaks up, requesting a change in the debate rules. What does he ask for?
5. Hoynes requests a private meeting with Josh. To discuss what?
6. Josh fires Amy. Why?
7. What are the names of the staffers from the Santos congressional office who are now part of his campaign?
8. Josh puts two volunteers in costumes to follow Russell and Hoynes and heckle them into joining the open debate. What kind of costumes?
9. Someone berates the volunteer following Russell, and is caught on camera doing so. Who?
10. Santos rejects a one-minute campaign TV spot Josh has made. What does he do instead?

"Drought Conditions"
S6/E16

As Vice President Russell settles into the lead in the race for the Democratic nomination, another dark horse candidate emerges – Sen. Ricky Rafferty, whose healthcare ideas sound suspiciously familiar to Josh. Toby has picked up a facial wound from a hands-on scuffle, a reflection and consequence of a personal tragedy he has suffered. CJ is trying to get support in Congress for a bill that isn't getting much love; she and Leo turn to a Republican for advice.

1. What is the personal tragedy that Toby has suffered?
2. What led to that tragedy?
3. What is CJ trying to get Congressional support for?
4. Who does she and Leo turn to for advice?
5. This Republican can be no help at all on the water bill; when asked why he bothered to come in and talk to them, what is his answer?
6. What does Leo tell her to do after their meeting?
7. Margaret spills coffee on CJ. How does CJ cover up the stain?
8. Who is Toby fighting when his face is injured?
9. Charlie mentions to Kate that a man at his gym asked about her. She expresses interest in going out with this man but suddenly changes her opinion. Why?
10. Someone provided Sen. Rafferty with inside information about the President's healthcare plans. Who?

"A Good Day"
S6/E17

Matt Santos steps off the campaign trail to support a crucial vote on a stem cell bill supported by the White House, only to find that Speaker Haffley is willing to go to nefarious lengths to see it fail. Toby unenthusiastically meets with a group of middle school students, only to get caught up in their enthusiasm when he hears them out. Kate is forced to deal with an impending invasion of Canada.

1. How does Speaker Haffley subvert the vote on the bill, which will pass with support from Congressional Democrats?
2. Cliff Calley has a weekly sporting engagement with Haffley, where he goads him into calling the vote. What sport?
3. A junior Congressional Democrat has doubts about the stem cell bill. What state is he from?
4. Where do the Congressional Democrats hide, in order to fake out Haffley?
5. What do the middle school students want to discuss with Toby?
6. What is the crisis in Canada that Kate has to deal with?
7. How does she bring the crises to an end?
8. What is she surprised to learn, in the process?
9. There is an older Japanese gentleman visiting the White House. Who is he, and why is he there?
10. This old Japanese gentleman injures himself. How?

"La Palabra"
S6/E18

The Santos campaign heads to California as Super Tuesday looms, intent on pushing his healthcare ideas. He is pressured to take a stand on a controversial issue. Whether or not to follow him to California is a consideration for the other two candidates. Donna takes on a new role with the Russell campaign.

1. Where in California does Santos go?
2. What is the controversial issue about which the press pressures Santos to take a stand?
3. Donna asks Will for something. What does he give her in response?
4. The Santos campaign is in danger. From what?
5. The Russell campaign suddenly decides to head for California. Why?
6. What solution do Santos and his wife entertain to solve the campaign's problems?
7. Matt and Helen Santos visit a California classroom. They are asked a curriculum-related question. What is it, and what is Santos's answer?
8. Ronna informs Santos, Josh and Helen that news is breaking about Hoynes. What news?
9. How does California's Governor Tillman handle the controversial bill?
10. Which candidate wins California in the primary?

"Ninety Miles Away"
S6/E19

Rumors of Fidel Castro's bad health prompt a covert mission to Cuba, prompting growls from a Florida senator. In flashback, two members of the Bartlet team are shown meeting in Cuba in the past.

1. The President reads from a book in Leo's office. Who is the author?
2. Who goes to Cuba and why?
3. What Florida senator has strong opinions about the Cuba situation?
4. Who does CJ send to talk to the senator?
5. The senator offers them something other than coffee. What?
6. The senator repeatedly references an administration official who was in Cuba in the past and, in his view, caused trouble. Who?
7. Charlie is preoccupied with an issue concerning the White House itself. What is it?
8. Which two Bartlet people met in Cuba in the past (though only one remembers the meeting)?
9. What year did that meeting occur?
10. The President and senior staff decide to address the nation and break the news of the secret talks with Castro in an address to the nation. What prompts them to do this?

"In God We Trust"
S6/E20

The Republicans have their nominee, and that nominee brings in a familiar face to run their campaign. The Democrats now head into their own convention with Russell in the lead, and Santos right behind, as a disgraced Hoynes hangs on for dear life.

1. Who is the Republican nominee?
2. Who is running their campaign?
3. Playing to the Evangelical Republican base, the nominee considers a famous evangelist as running mate. What is the evangelist's name?
4. Who eventually is selected as the Republican VP candidate?
5. Why does the Republican nominee require a devout running mate?
6. The President brings Santos and Russell in to the White House for a photo op, then privately makes something clear. What does he say to them?
7. On what major issue does the Republican nominee break with the party?
8. The Majority Leader calls the Republican nominee and urges him to meet with President Bartlet to get him to change a piece of legislation. What is the legislation, and what is the change?
9. The Republican nominee, asking that the President spend a little extra time with him so that it looks like they haggled, ends up in the White House kitchen with him. They have a snack; what is it?
10. While they have their snack, they have a discussion; about what?

"Things Fall Apart"
S6/E21

Compared to the Republican Convention, the Democrats look utterly disorganized with the three candidates blocking each other from a majority of delegates. President Bartlet seeks to bring at least a little order to the process by sending Leo to oversee it. Overhead, the International Space Station is leaking oxygen, endangering the lives of three astronauts.

1. Bob Russell meets with someone to discuss the vice presidential spot on the ticket. Who?
2. Will pitches that same position to someone else. Who?
3. CJ is briefed on the space station crisis by a NASA administrator. How long do the astronauts have before they run out of air?
4. In briefing CJ, the NASA administrator alludes to a possible rescue scenario, but knowledge of it is classified. What is it?
5. Charlie and the President have an awkward moment. What is the nature of the awkwardness?
6. CJ discusses the NASA administrator's allusion with another senior staffer. Who?
7. Leo takes Josh aside and tells him he must do something. What?
8. A member of the Russell campaign advises Josh that Santos should reject the offer of the VP slot. Who?
9. Arnold Vinick, accepting the Republican nomination, does something unexpected in his speech. What does he say?
10. A member of the White House press corps is putting out a story about the space station crisis and the classified rescue option. Who is the reporter and what paper do they write for?

"2162 Votes"
S6/E22

The Democratic National Convention begins, and it's the free-for-mess that Bartlet and Leo had feared. At the White House, an even greater problem is what to do about the astronauts aboard the ISS.

1. Josh attempts to shake up the home stretch to the nomination by approaching one of the other candidates. Which one, and what does he say?
2. Gov. Baker is offered the VP slot by Russell. He does something else instead. What?
3. Josh realizes that Santos cannot win without a particular group's support, and that support would bring delegates What group is it?
4. Josh meets with that group's leader, who objects to a policy Santos has proposed that his group does not like. What is the policy?
5. Who finally sways that leader to endorse Santos?
6. Information surfaces that could damage Baker, but Santos isn't interested in using it. What is it?
7. Josh has failed to convince Santos to stand aside for Russell. Someone else tries; who?
8. As the convention drags on, the President still hasn't decided who he should endorse. Someone urges him to set political expediency aside and choose the one he really wants. Who does this?
9. The FBI tells Kate Harper something about its investigation of the secret space shuttle incident. What do they tell her?
10. Getting the nomination, Santos then names a VP. Who is it?

SEASON 6 EPISODE QUIZ ANSWERS

S6E1: "NSF Thurmont"
1. Admiral Fitzwallace
2. Belfast, Ireland
3. She developed a pulmonary embolism
4. "NICE HAT"
5. "SCARED"
6. Leo wants to strike both the Palestinians and Iran; the President doesn't want to strike either
7. a Congressional resolution
8. He's predictable
9. Eli Zahavy
10. Naval Support Facility Thurmont is the formal name of Camp David, the presidential retreat

S6E2: "The Birnam Wood"
1. An attack on the terrorists' training camp in Syria
2. The disposition of Jerusalem
3. Josh, returning from Germany
4. basketball
5. Leo
6. The right of Palestinians, ousted from the territory that became Israel in 1947, to resettle in their homeland
7. a Shabat dinner
8. directing evening prayers toward Mecca
9. Kate Harper
10. Leo suffers a massive heart attack in the woods surrounding the camp, after being fired by the President

S6E3: "Third-Day Story"
1. A swim test
2. If he completes his degree, he must keep his promise to the President to stop working for him and move on with his future
3. in the woods surrounding Camp David

4. a tax cut
5. eating junk food
6. cook him dinner
7. the child tax credit; they agree to different numbers of eligible children per family, creating confusion
8. Who will be the new White House Chief of Staff?
9. Greg Brock (of the *New York Times*)
10. CJ; "jump off a cliff"

S6E4: "Liftoff"
1. Toby, Josh, and President Bartlet
2. They pretend to resign
3. enriched uranium
4. a Tiger Team
5. Secretary of State Miles Hutchinson
6. running for a Connecticut seat in Congress, taking an executive role at the DCCC
7. Matt Santos
8. Texas
9. The Patient's Bill of Rights
10. Annabeth Schott

S6E5: "The Hubbert Peak"
1. an oversized SUV
2. It is environmentally unfriendly
3. He crashes it
4. He went to the dealership intending to check out an environment-friendly Prius – and crashes the SUV into a Prius
5. the discovery of oil in any particular area
6. representatives for the solar, wind, hydrogen and ethanol industries
7. make the President play chess
8. stick it in a drawer and ignore it
9. Deputy Special Assistant to the Chief of Staff
10. "rats of unusual size"; *The Princess Bride*

S6E6: "The Dover Test"

1. "The Secretary of Agriculture is in the Rose Room"
2. He is going to break ranks and join with a Republican on the Patient's Bill of Rights
3. That he didn't notify the Vice President's office that Santos was breaking ranks on the bill
4. the soldier's father hangs up on Debbie before the President even gets on the line
5. a measure of public support falling as a function of military coffins arriving at Dover Air Force Base
6. an administration policy keeping the press away from Dover AFB
7. His nurse appears, urgently looking for him, telegraphing to his friend that he is convalescing
8. running Bob Russell for President
9. Have the President visit the wounded at Walter Reed
10. While posturing over breaking ranks, he renegotiated the entire bill in ways favoring Democratic priorities

S6E7: "A Change is Gonna Come"

1. a flag representing the Taiwanese Independence Movement, which is offensive to China
2. China is against Taiwanese independence; their delegation, in talks with the White House about the President's visit, gets up and walks out
3. Curtis
4. "Josh – Time to lead – John"
5. at the National Prayer Breakfast
6. Bernard Thatch
7. Gov. Eric Baker
8. Vice President Russell
9. He didn't see it, due to an MS-related weakening of his eyes
10. James Taylor

S6E8: "In the Room"

1. Zoey Bartlet's birthday
2. Penn and Teller

3. They make an American flag appear to vanish in a burst of flame
4. Josh; that they reveal how they did the trick, so that people will not think a flag was burned in the White House
5. Surgeon General Millie Griffith
6. Republican Sen. Arnold Vinick
7. shining his shoes
8. POTUS
9. Gov. Eric Baker
10. from a wheelchair

S6E9: "Impact Winter"
1. Vice President Russell
2. playing tennis
3. the Cabinet will be meeting
4. Abbey
5. 48 hours
6. her future in her role at the White House
7. Taiwan and North Korea
8. Marla
9. Houston
10. Matt Santos

S6E10: "Faith-Based Initiative"
1. staffer on the Russell campaign
2. Wilkinson
3. He wants a provision banning gay marriage added to the budget bill
4. Vice President Russell
5. John Hoynes
6. Matt Santos
7. that Josh manage his campaign
8. Todd
9. "the most powerful lesbian on the planet"
10. that it's none of anyone's business

S6E11: "Opposition Research"

1. his education plan
2. Elizabeth (Liz) Bartlet
3. Greg Brock of the *New York Times*
4. That the Santos education plan has been leaked to the Associated Press, and that an old, controversial Santos quote about the New Hampshire primary has surfaced
5. Joey Lucas
6. Josh himself
7. opposition research
8. Santos himself
9. a contribution to the Santos campaign, which will become public record
10. Will

S6E12: "365 Days"

1. In CJ's old office
2. North Korea has "poked a hole in the fence"
3. a protest in Bolivia, in which US contractors have been taken captive
4. the Earned Income Tax Credit, which needs a better name
5. unemployment
6. a NASCAR race
7. in the residence, napping
8. when Bolivian elections are allowed to proceed
9. a ceremonial kiss from the winning NASCAR driver
10. it has moved an inch

S6E13: "King Corn"

1. 5 a.m.
2. "taking the pledge"
3. Arnold Vinick
4. immigration
5. Helen
6. Sheila (Brooks)
7. Bob (Mayer)

8. Ned (Carlson)
9. Helen Santos
10. over a table in the hotel dining room on the evening after their ethanol speeches

S6E14: "The Wake Up Call"
1. Kate Harper
2. Prof. Lawrence Lessig
3. Belarus
4. Valentine's Day
5. Bhutan
6. bomb several Iranian nuclear plants
7. He had stayed up past midnight chatting with Prof. Lessig
8. Abbey
9. The Iranians misidentified the British plane as a US spy plane
10. Maureen Graty

S6E15: "Freedonia"
1. It is a fictional country in a Marx Brothers comedy; it is mentioned in the episode as having been brought up in a Senate debate where a senator actually claimed to be studying it, but the debate rules didn't allow him to be challenged
2. Santos hires her to help him with the "presidential voice".
3. He realizes he will do better in an open debate than one-on-one against Hoynes
4. that the candidates be allowed to directly address each other
5. He and Santos put out identical statements on Pakistan, and he tells Josh that if they're going to use the same material, they should tweak it so it's not obvious
6. Ned (Carlson) and Ronna (Beckman)
7. for leaking the Pakistan material to other candidates
8. chicken costumes
9. Donna
10. goes to a local station and speaks on air live for one minute about why people should vote for him

S6E16: "Drought Conditions"

1. His brother David has died
2. He had terminal cancer and took his own life
3. a water bill involving resources in the Western US
4. Cliff Calley, the Republican attorney who helped protect Leo during the Congressional inquiry into the MS scandal, who is now a lobbyist
5. He wants a box of M&Ms with the Seal of the President on them
6. He tells her to hire Calley as Deputy Chief of Staff
7. by wearing Margaret's blazer
8. Josh
9. She realizes the man is her ex-husband
10. Toby

S6E17: "A Good Day"

1. By refusing to call the vote while there are sufficient Democrats in town to ensure its passage
2. squash
3. Arkansas
4. Vice President Russell's office
5. lowering the voting age
6. American hunters have been surrounded by Canadian ranchers across the border
7. by threatening to cancel hunting season and start revoking licenses
8. that the US does in fact have invasion plans for Canada
9. Dr. Yosh Takahashi; he shared the Nobel Prize with President Bartlet, and is there to attend a dinner honoring Nobel Laureates
10. trying to do a tango

S6E18: "La Palabra"

1. Sacramento
2. a bill in California that would deny driver's licenses to illegal immigrants
3. more responsibility; she becomes the campaign spokeswoman
4. The money is running out

5. Donna realizes that the Hoynes campaign doesn't intend to go to California, so it would be a mistake for Russell not to exploit that absence and gain momentum there
6. mortgaging their home to generate some additional funds
7. Would he support the teaching of Creationism in science classes? No; Creationism isn't science
8. that a scandal has just broken in which Hoynes is accused of sexual misconduct
9. He vetoes it, with Santos standing beside him as he announces the veto
10. Santos

S6E19: "Ninety Miles Away"
1. Ernest Hemingway
2. Leo, to have covert talks about lifting outdated embargos
3. Sen. Rafe Framhagen
4. Cliff Calley
5. orange juice – with a shot of vodka, if he prefers
6. Kate Harper
7. an infestation of bugs
8. Leo and Kate
9. 1995
10. Cuban-American factions are going to break the news anyway

S6E20: "In God We Trust"
1. Sen. Arnold Vinick
2. Bruno Gianelli
3. Rev. Don Butler
4. West Virginia Gov. Ray Sullivan
5. He doesn't attend church
6. They'd better keep it clean, and if one of them doesn't, he will likely endorse the other
7. abortion
8. The debt ceiling bill; the Republicans want a minimum wage amendment removed
9. some ice cream

10. whether or not a president's religious beliefs or practices are the public's business

S6E21: "Things Fall Apart"
1. Gov. Eric Baker of Pennsylvania
2. He meets with Josh to say that Russell will give Santos the VP spot in exchange for his delegates
3. 3 weeks
4. A military space shuttle exists but its existence is top secret
5. Charlie runs into the President while slipping out of Zoey's bedroom late at night
6. Toby
7. Get Santos to accept Russell's VP offer
8. Donna
9. He praises President Bartlet
10. Greg Brock; the *New York Times*

S6E22: "2162 Votes"
1. Hoynes; Josh attempts to get him to stand down and give his delegates to Santos
2. He attempts to get nominated from the convention floor
3. the Teachers' Union
4. bringing an end to teacher tenure
5. President Bartlet
6. private information about his wife's depression and medication
7. Leo
8. CJ
9. They believe they have learned the identity of the leaker
10. Leo

"The Ticket"
S7/E1

Flashforward beyond the Bartlet Administration, where a reunion takes place and the President's successor is teased but not identified. Back in the present, the Santos campaign refocuses on running against Vinick. Santos has concerns about Leo as a VP candidate; in the White House, Counsel Oliver Babish begins looking into the NASA leak.

1. How far forward is this flash?
2. Where does this reunion happen, and what's the event?
3. Who is seen at this reunion?
4. Who joins the group at the end of the scene?
5. The President passes on a request from Abbey; what is it?
6. Toby is now a professor; at what school?
7. Will is now a congressman, and mentions a committee he is serving on; what committee?
8. Someone has taken on the task of grooming Leo as a candidate. Who?
9. Joey Lucas, through her interpreter Kenny, offers a colorful adjective to describe Santos. What is it?
10. In this episode, we learn that someone has had a baby. Who?

"The Mommy Problem"
S7/E2

The Santos campaign gets a new team member, a none-too-delicate media consultant that gives Josh pause. Needing to shake up the campaign, the team debates whether or not Santos should stay quiet about the Bartlet Administration's decision not to investigate itself over the NASA leak.

1. What is the media consultant's name?
2. White House reporter Greg Brock is in big trouble. Why?
3. Frustrated at Vinick's pushing-back on security as an issue that the Santos team must deal with, Josh calls the White House to vent. At whom?
4. Someone named Bill introduces himself to Josh at Santos campaign headquarters. Josh assumes him to be a new staffer and leads him to an office. But he is there, in fact, to _____?
5. Two pop/rock legends are mentioned in a comparison of Vinick and Santos. Which two, and which one does Josh like?
6. Santos's status as a military reservist leads to a photo that makes the news which reinforces the Santos campaign's national security message. What does the photo show?
7. After meeting Santos, the media consultant agrees to join the campaign as Director of Communications, on one condition. What is it?
8. A second photo, released by the Associated Press, could be potentially scandalous to the Santos campaign. What does this photo show?
9. What comment does Santos make to the press with regard to the photo?
10. What does "the Mommy Problem" refer to?

"Message of the Week"
S7/E3

Arnold Vinick hits back hard after the Santos campaign's surge, attempting to force Santos into a corner on the issue of immigration. He has trouble on his own side of the fence as some of his supporters on the religious right insist on input into judicial appointments.

1. Vinick appears on a real-world news show with a real-world news host. What is the show and who is the host?
2. What is Vinick's Secret Service codename?
3. A man introduces himself to Vinick and tells him he will be giving him daily intelligence briefings. What is his name?
4. Who is running the Vinick campaign?
5. The Vinick team reviews a television spot and makes a decision about the tone of the campaign. What is it?
6. A religious group has a meeting with Vinick. What is the name of the group?
7. This group is very demanding; they try to insist that Vinick travel to what city in order to speak with them?
8. Vinick is forced to meet with a Republican political operative he doesn't like very much. What's his name?
9. That meeting leads to a report in the media that backs Vinick into a corner he very much doesn't want to be in. Where does the report surface, and what does it say?
10. Vinick is asked about a militia group that patrols the Texas-Mexico border. What is the name of the group?

"Mr. Frost"
S7/E4

Flashforward beyond the Bartlet Administration, where a reunion takes place and the President's successor is teased but not identified.

1. Which Bartlet staffer testifies before a Senate committee on the NASA leak?
2. What Palestinian leader is assassinated?
3. How was he killed?
4. On the campaign trail, Matt Santos is asked a question about the teaching of intelligent design in public schools. He gives a whimsical, quotable answer. What is it?
5. Josh is alarmed by what Santos said. He calls the comment "Creationism _____"?
6. Two others mention being served with a subpoena to appear before the Senate committee. Who are they?
7. Charlie escorts a messenger to someone else to serve yet another subpoena. To whom?
8. Lou keeps getting Ned's name wrong. What does she call him?
9. Who is the focus of the investigation into the NASA leak?
10. At the end of the episode, someone confesses to being the leaker. Who is it, and to whom do they confess?

"Here Today"
S7/E5

Toby's self-outing as the NASA leaker sets a somber tone as an angry President Bartlet responds to the revelation. Lou is concerned that the Santos campaign needs big, visible changes. CIA official Charles Frost earns Kate's wrath.

1. CJ summons someone from the White House Counsel's office to her own, to formally deal with Toby's confession. Who is it?
2. Oliver Babish begins interviewing Toby about his leaking of the NASA information. Someone interrupts the interview and shuts it down. Who?
3. How much jail time is Toby told he's facing, if convicted?
4. Someone besides Chairman Farad has been assassinated. Who?
5. Helen Santos is watching a horror film aboard the campaign plane, starring what real-world singer/actor?
6. Ellie brings her fiancé to the West Wing. What is his name?
7. What does the President call him?
8. Toby offers the President his resignation; how many does that make?
9. President Bartlet rejects his resignation, saying that he must do something else instead. What?
10. Oliver Babish says Toby is due for something; what?

"The Al Smith Dinner"
S7/E6

Flashforward beyond the Bartlet Administration, where a reunion takes place and the President's successor is teased but not identified.

1. Who shows up at the Santos campaign, wanting to join?
2. Who ends up hiring that person?
3. The "Al Smith Dinner" is a real-world thing. What is it?
4. Arnold Vinick wants to skip the dinner, because he knows a topic that's dicey for him is sure to come up. What is it?
5. Who takes Toby's old job, becoming the new White House Director of Communications?
6. An attack ad on Santos is released, prompting him to insist that Vinick repudiate it, or face the campaign going negative. Who is actually responsible for the ad?
7. Vinick is pressured to embrace the attack ad by those who released it. What is his response?
8. A Santos campaign staffer meets with Bruno Gianelli to discuss debates, only not really. Who is it?
9. Vinick and Santos meet at the Al Smith Dinner. Where, specifically?
10. In that private meeting, they come to an agreement. To do what?

"The Debate"
S7/E7

In an actual live broadcast (one for each US coast, actually), the two candidates debate in real time.

1. What real-world media journalist moderates the debate?
2. As the debate begins, Vinick makes an astonishing proposal, to which Santos and the moderator agree. What it is?
3. Vinick suggests that the solution to the Mexican border problem is to do what?
4. Santos counters by suggesting something else, to demonstrate the futility of Vinick's solution. What?
5. Santos says his ideal solution to millions of Americans not having healthcare is to do what?
6. Vinick opposes the re-importing of American drugs from Canada at cheaper prices. Why?
7. Vinick also claims that debt relief isn't the solution to poverty in poor African countries. What is his solution?
8. Santos embraces with pride a political label served up by Vinick as a put-down, offering the debate audience a litany of the accomplishments, over time, of those so identified. What is that label?
9. Santos proposes a radical solution to gun control. Instead of "gun control", he favors _____?
10. Santos makes a pledge to the audience, and encourages Vinick to join him in that pledge (which he doesn't). What is the pledge?

"Undecideds"
S7/E8

Santos takes the controversial step of visiting the family of a slain Los Angeles black boy who was shot by police. At the White House, Ellie and Vic plan their wedding.

1. The major news outlets rendered verdicts on the outcome of the debate. How did they call it?
2. How old was the black boy who was killed?
3. What detail about the shooting makes Santos visiting the community problematic?
4. Where are Ellie and Vic getting married?
5. CJ hands off the task of helping them with their wedding plans. Who gets the job?
6. CJ's handoff happens because Kate Harper informs her of an international incident developing. Between which three countries?
7. The incident involves a partnership between two of the countries to build something. Which two countries, building what?
8. What seafood entrée do Margeret and CJ agree to push for the wedding dinner?
9. What is Santos's dilemma, as he prepares to speak at a black church about the shooting?
10. Where is President Bartlet while all this is going on?

"The Wedding"
S7/E9

The big day has arrived for presidential daughter Ellie Bartlet and her fiancé Vic, as the President deals with the escalation of the China-Russia incident. The Santos campaign has a staffing change.

1. As President Bartlet does the wedding rehearsal walk-through with Abbey and Ellie, he is interrupted. Who interrupts him, and why?
2. Santos does a photo op with Gov. Baker in Philadelphia, and has an accident. What is it?
3. A senator approaches Josh and chides him for not getting the campaign into a Midwestern state sooner than it did. Which state?
4. The senator also advises Josh to put money back into a state he's pulling out of. Which state?
5. Who does Kate ask to be her plus-one for the wedding?
6. The President has a man-to-man talk with Vic. Where does this talk take place?
7. Vic tells the President the point in his relationship when he knew he wanted to marry her. What point was that?
8. The DNC chairman is in town, and is interested in serious talks with the Santos team about the final stretch of the campaign. What is his name?
9. With all the bigwigs in town for the wedding, some staffers have quietly taken up a game, to amuse themselves. What is it?
10. Who does the DNC chair think can manage the Santos campaign better than Josh?

"Running Mates"
S7/E10

It's Leo's turn at bat, with the Vice Presidential debate. After seeing his performance in prep, the campaign staff is very concerned. The Santos family gets a lesson in presidential security.

1. Leo will be debating Republican Vice Presidential candidate Ray Sullivan. Which Santos campaign staffer stands in for Sullivan during debate prep?
2. The tape of the mock debate is so bad that Josh doesn't dare let Leo see it. What does he do to prevent it?
3. What is Santos's son's name?
4. Annabeth, coaching Leo, tells him he must work on his "default expression". What is that default expression?
5. Leo disagrees, and calls his default expression something else. What?
6. The Secret Service protection around the Santos home is so strict that even a family member has trouble getting in. What family member?
7. An embarrassing photo of Helen Santos appears in a tabloid. What does it show?
8. Will and Kate have an actual dinner date. Where do they have dinner?
9. Leo turns in a winning performance in the debate; his strategy going in was to lower expectations. How did he achieve that?
10. Leo sends email from Annabeth's laptop by guessing her password, which is a name. What name?

"Internal Displacement"
S7/E11

CJ works to negotiate with Russian and China to prevent war. Embarrassing information about a member of the President's family comes to her attention, as Josh urges the White House to let Santos announce the building of a research facility in Texas.

1. CJ meets someone for dinner. Who?
2. CJ gets a tip about a member of the President's family. Which member?
3. The tip involves a rumor. What is the rumor?
4. Who does CJ assign to investigate the rumor?
5. What is the research facility that Josh wants Santos to announce?
6. How much federal funding is going to the building of the lab?
7. CJ is hesitant to allow Josh to make the lab announcement, because it will endanger the re-election bid of a senator who will be held in disfavor by his constituents for failing to get it for his own state. Which state?
8. CJ meets with three ambassadors over violence in the Sudan. Ambassadors of which countries?
9. Where in Texas will the new lab be built?
10. "So, if I'm going to jump off the cliff, and you're going to be pushed off the cliff - _____?

"Duck and Cover"
S7/E12

A nuclear reactor breaks in Southern California, triggering a major crisis as tens of thousands of people flee and the President musters a federal response. Both Santos and Vinick must likewise cope with the disaster – Vinick in particular, as it is happening in his home state. Kate Harper continues to deal with the tense situation over Kazakhstan.

1. In what community is the nuclear reactor located?
2. What is the population of that community (how many people are in danger)?
3. Matt Santos professed a liking for a classic rock figure. Who?
4. What media source did he reveal this liking to?
5. Which two albums by this classic rocker did he cite? Which one is his favorite?
6. Speaking derisively of Santos's appearance at a Rock the Vote rally, Bruno Gianelli calls Santos _____?
7. San Andreo is close to what major, heavily-populated California city?
8. The nuclear reactor crisis is particularly precarious for Vinick, and not just because he is the senior senator from California. What's the other reason?
9. President Bartlet sends engineers into the radioactive plant to restore the cooling system. How many are killed in the process?
10. How long does the first team of engineers remain in the plant?

"The Cold"
S7/E13

The Russia-China crisis grows ever more serious, prompting President Bartlet to bring Vinick and Santos in from the campaign trail so he can brief them, just as the polls are getting interesting in the aftermath of the San Andreo crisis. Josh and Donna have an unprecedented moment.

1. What do the polls say about the Vinick-Santos race?
2. Donna goes to Josh's hotel room to break the news about the polls. What happens next?
3. Will has something of Kate's, and needs to return it discreetly. What is it?
4. Stoked over the polls, the Santos campaign heads for a state where they hope to take the lead. Which state?
5. How many US troops is the President considering sending to Kazakhstan?
6. The President is concerned that the troops he sends will need some very specific provisioning. What does he tell Secretary Hutchinson they will need?
7. A real-world rock star wants to have dinner with Santos. Who?
8. Another real-world rocker is at a Santos campaign rally; Santos mentions that he is going to proceed him on state. Who is it?
9. Vinick and Santos divert to the White House for a briefing on Kazakhstan. Josh is asked to bring Leo along, and demurs. Who calls Josh to make sure he brings Leo?
10. There is a shake-up at the Vinick campaign. To adjust perceptions, an RNC operative is brought in to replace a campaign staffer. Which staffer, and who is the replacement?

"Two Weeks Out"
S7/E14

With two weeks left before the election, Vinick defies his campaign advisors to take a stand in his home state.

1. Vinick is struggling physically. What is his issue?
2. Both candidates appear in a major Midwestern city. Which one?
3. Someone is helping Josh behind the scenes, and urges him to get Santos out to California ASAP. Who?
4. How does Vinick think he should deal with the press regarding the San Andreo nuclear accident (against his campaign staff's advise)?
5. What does Vinick call the event he proposes?
6. Which campaign advisor threatens to quit over Vinick's decision?
7. Something belonging to Santos has gone missing. What?
8. Who finds the thing that Santos is missing?
9. This thing is compromising to Santos. How?
10. Vinick privately confronts Santos about it. What is the explanation?

"Welcome to Wherever You Are"
S7/E15

Flashforward beyond the Bartlet Administration, where a.

1. What real-world rock star is aboard the Santos campaign bus?
2. What musical instrument does Matt Santos play?
3. Toby is under indictment already, but another indictment is threatened if he doesn't give up his source. Who was Toby's source?
4. What is the new threatened indictment for?
5. Who is threatening Toby with the indictment?
6. Toby is further threatened; if he doesn't give up his source, someone else will be indicted. Who?
7. Someone close to Toby lobbies hard to get him to reveal David as his source. Who?
8. It's a holiday, and the Santos family is celebrating a holiday ritual before the cameras of the press. What holiday?
9. An embarrassing event occurs before the cameras. What happens?
10. Helen Santos expresses a controversial opinion that is picked up by the press, stressing out her husband. On what issue?

"Election Day (Pt. I)"
S7/E16

It's Election Day, finally, after a very long and difficult campaign for both sides. As voting begins across the nation, tragedy strikes.

1. On the night before Election Day, the Santos campaign staff gathers in a bar for drinks. Two by two, they slip away, pairing off for election night sex. Who leaves as Lou leaves?
2. Josh and Donna are left alone. What happens next?
3. Charlie gets CJ thinking about something. What?
4. As the Santos team watches votes roll in, Josh is stricken with anxiety over something that makes no sense to him; what?
5. A real-world rock band is featured, performing for the Santos campaign. What band?
6. Josh is encouraged to do something for the campaign staff, and ends up doing the opposite. What is it?
7. A member of the Bartlet team votes for Vinick. Which one?
8. A beloved character dies. Who?
9. How do they die?
10. Who finds them?

"Election Day (Pt. II)"
S7/E17

Leo McGarry's death goes public, overshadowing the election in progress. The candidates are neck-and-neck, right down to the wire.

1. Rushing to the hospital, Josh and Donna are briefly stuck in an elevator. A Stevie Wonder song is playing. What song?
2. The Santos campaign weighs speaking out publicly about Leo's death. Who wants to speak out? Who advises against it?
3. Who breaks the news to President Bartlet?
4. Who calls Arnold Vinick to tell him Leo has died?
5. Who wins Texas?
6. Who wins California?
7. The election comes down to two states: which two?
8. As Santos was pressured to not speak up about Leo's death, Vinick is also under pressure. What does he refuse to do?
9. At one point, the Santos team breaks into song. What song?
10. When the winner is declared, President Bartlet has already gone to bed. Who wakes him to announce the winner?

"Requiem"
S7/E18

Leo is gone, and his family, friends and colleagues gather to say goodbye. .

1. Name as many familiar faces as you can from Leo's funeral service?
2. Name Leo's six pallbearers?
3. Toby hangs back in the cathedral as it empties, wary of the press. Who appears to stand with him as he leaves?
4. Josh is knocked off-balance when Santos doesn't appoint him to head the transition team. Who gets the job instead?
5. Several staffers who knew Leo best gather in the White House residence with the President and Abbey to reminisce about Leo, in which much personal information about Leo emerges. What kind of suits did he wear?
6. Per Annabeth, Leo's peach shirts were actually _____?
7. People start turning up at the White House, looking for jobs in the new administration. One of them is Ainsley Hayes. What job does she want?
8. Where has Ainsley been working?
9. Santos has Amy Gardner in mind for what job?
10. Who selflessly offers to be Santos's vice president?

"Transition"
S7/E19

Following the election and Leo's funeral, the new administration starts transitioning into the White House. An old familiar face reappears, and Bartlet staffers find themselves in new roles, with new options.

1. Josh heads to Los Angeles. To see who?
2. What do they say to Josh when they see him?
3. He offers an administration position to them. What is it?
4. Donna gives Josh an ultimatum. What is it?
5. Donna gets a job offer. For what job?
6. Josh, stressed from nearly a year on the campaign trail, takes the head off a staffer. Which one?
7. CJ is furious when Santos calls a foreign head of state, serving up a policy position at odds with President Bartlet's. It's the head of state of what country?
8. CJ's fury is misplaced; why?
9. While many campaign staffers want positions in the new administration, Josh has to lobby one of them really hard. Who?
10. Josh departs Washington for a much-needed week of vacation. Who does he take with him?

"The Last Hurrah"
S7/E20

As President-elect Santos begins pulling his incoming administration together, Arnold Vinick is at loose ends.

1. Santos and his wife duck out of the transition office to tour a few places. What are they?
2. Santos and his wife also throw the Secret Service a major curve ball, causing a momentary disruption in transition planning. What is it?
3. CJ introduces Helen Santos to the White House domestic staff. Helen protests that there are too many of them. What does CJ then ask her?
4. When Vinick's staffers hear his post-election plans, they begin to suspect he is preparing for something. What?
5. Vinick, getting some coffee in a coffee shop, is faced with his relative anonymity when the counter person gets his name wrong. What does he call him?
6. Who does Santos want as his vice president?
7. Santos offers Vinick a position in his administration. In what role?
8. Who questions Santos on making that offer?
9. Who among the Democrats tells Vinick he'd be doing them a favor if he turned down Santos's offer?
10. Who lobbies Vinick hard to accept the offer?

"Institutional Memory"
S7/E21

As the Santos inauguration draws closer, Bartlet staffers consider their options – both professional and personal.

1. Everybody wants to hire CJ. What astonishing offer does she receive, and who makes the offer?
2. Who else makes CJ an offer?
3. Will Bailey gets an offer. From whom, to do what?
4. Will gets an idea, while pondering the next round of Congressional races. What is it?
5. Andy Wyatt appears at the White House to ask CJ for a favor. What is it?
6. CJ sneaks an incendiary initiative into the final Bartlet budget to make Santos look good. What is it?
7. CJ visits Toby, and he tells her he has found something remarkable. What is it?
8. CJ is anxious as she speaks to Toby. What is causing her anxiety?
9. CJ sees Danny, who asks her two questions that clear up her hesitations. What are they?
10. CJ finally makes two choices – one professional, one personal. What are they?

"Tomorrow"
S7/E22

The Bartlet Administration comes to an end as Matt Santos takes the oath of office. Decisions about the future are made by many.

1. Who gets Debbie Fiderer's job as Executive Secretary?
2. Mallory drops in on CJ to leave a gift for her to pass on to President Bartlet. What is it?
3. Josh drops by CJ's office before the inauguration. She hands him a note. What does it say?
4. With nothing else to do, three Bartlet staffers discuss going to the movies. Which three?
5. Who gets Charlie's office, which was Annabeth's office, which was Will's office, and originally Sam's office?
6. What is President Bartlet's final act as president?
7. A face famous and beloved by *West Wing* fans is seen in the inauguration crowd. Who is it?
8. What song is performed at the inauguration?
9. As President Santos takes his place behind his Oval Office desk, three staffers are facing him. Which three?
10. The episode's title is the answer to a question. What is the question, who asks it, who are they asking, and where are they when it is asked?

SEASON 7 EPISODE QUIZ ANSWERS

S7E1: "The Ticket"
1. Three years
2. The Bartlet Presidential Library; it is the day of its dedication
3. CJ, Danny Concannon, Toby, Kate, Charlie, and Will
4. Josh
5. She wants a picture of Danny and CJ's baby
6. Columbia
7. Ways and Means
8. Annabeth
9. "hunky"
10. Leo's daughter Mallory

S7E2: "The Mommy Problem"
1. Louise (Lou) Thornton
2. for refusing to answer a grand jury's questions about how he learned of the space station leak and military shuttle
3. CJ
4. install some new phone lines
5. Neil Young, Neil Diamond; Josh is a fan of the latter
6. a photo of Matt Santos in a flight suit on an air base tarmac, flanked by two other pilots
7. that she reports directly to Santos, rather than to Josh
8. a bed that collapsed while Santos and his wife were having sex in it
9. "No way was that bed steel-reinforced!"
10. Josh: "When voters want a national daddy, someone to be tough and strong and defend the country; when they want a mommy, someone to give them jobs, healthcare... they vote Democratic."

S7E3: "Message of the Week"
1. *Hardball* with Chris Matthews
2. Big Sur
3. Charles Frost
4. Bruno Gianelli

5. that they won't go negative
6. the American Christian Assembly
7. Atlanta, GA
8. George Rohr
9. The Drudge Report: "VINICK PROMISES PRO-LIFE JUDGES"
10. The Minutemen

S7E4: "Mr. Frost"
1. Margaret (Hooper)
2. Chairman Farad
3. a suicide bombing
4. "I believe in God, and I like to think he's intelligent."
5. "Creationism with a Groucho mask"
6. Leo and Toby
7. Charlie
8. Ted
9. CJ
10. Toby, to CJ

S7E5: "Here Today"
1. Mike Wayne
2. Alana Waterman, Toby's attorney
3. "63 to 78 months," or roughly "six years"
4. Kazakhstan's President Issanov
5. Rob Zombie
6. Vic Faison
7. "the Fruit Fly Guy"
8. 3
9. he must fire him, for cause
10. Someone should thank him for his service

S7E6: "The Al Smith Dinner"
1. Donna
2. Lou hires her, after Josh refuses to

3. A Catholic charities benefit established in honor of the first Catholic to run for president in 1928; presidential nominees still attend, to this day
4. abortion; Vinick breaks with the Republican party in being pro-choice
5. Will
6. The Republican National Committee
7. that if the RNC does not denounce the ad, he'll have to do it himself
8. Lou
9. in the kitchen behind the auditorium where the dinner is being held
10. to have an old-school debate

S7E7: "The Debate"
1. Forrest Sawyer
2. that they abandon their agreed-upon rules for the debate and have an open debate instead
3. double the border patrol
4. triple the border patrol – which had already been done, to little effect
5. make Medicare available to all
6. He says the practice is unfair to the US pharmaceutical industry
7. tax cuts
8. "liberal"
9. "bullet control"
10. that he will never go to war over oil

S7E8: "Undecideds"
1. a tie
2. 12
3. the police officer who shot the boy was Latino
4. the White House
5. Will
6. China, Russia, and Kazakhstan
7. China and Kazakhstan; an oil pipeline between their countries

8. trout
9. whether or not to denounce the Latino police officer
10. Camp David, with a South American delegation, working on a trade agreement

S7E9: "The Wedding"
1. CJ; the China/Russia/Kazakhstan situation is escalating, with three Russian convoys headed for the border
2. He has a cheesesteak sandwich, and spills cheese whiz all over his shirt
3. Illinois
4. Iowa
5. Will
6. The Oval Office
7. on their 3rd date
8. Barry Goodwin
9. Dignitary Bingo
10. Leo

S7E10: "Running Mates"
1. Otto
2. He destroys the tape and tells Leo that the tape machine ate it
3. Peter
4. a smirk
5. a scowl
6. Jorge Santos, his brother
7. Helen Santos bending over, with the strap of a thong showing
8. at Will's desk in his office, complete with tablecloth and candles
9. by leaking word of his poor performance to the press
10. her cat's name

S7E11: "Internal Displacement"
1. Danny Concannon
2. his son-in-law, Doug Westin
3. that he is sleeping with the family nanny

4. Will
5. a molecular transport lab
6. $2 billion
7. Kentucky
8. France, Germany, and China
9. Austin
10. "Why don't we hold hands on the way down?"

S7E12: "Duck and Cover"
1. San Andreo
2. 42,000
3. Bob Dylan
4. *Rolling Stone*
5. *Highway 61 Revisited, Blonde on Blonde*; the latter is his favorite
6. "a latter-day Mick Jagger-in-Chief"
7. San Diego
8. He lobbied hard for federal approval of the reactor 25 years earlier
9. 1
10. 32 minutes

S7E13: "The Cold"
1. Vinick and Santos are tied, nationally
2. they kiss
3. a bra
4. California
5. 150,000
6. Outerwear; coats: it is very, very cold in Kazakhstan
7. Bono (of U2)
8. Dave Matthews
9. President Bartlet
10. Sheila; Jane Braun

S7E14: "Two Weeks Out"
1. His hand is very sore; shaking hands is deeply painful
2. Chicago

3. Toby
4. Go to the San Andreo plant and hold a press conference, facing questions directly until they pack up and leave
5. a "Til They Drop" press conference
6. Jane Braun
7. his personal briefcase
8. Bruno
9. a checkbook recording payments made to a woman named Anita Morales, who has a child that Bruno and Vinick assumes to be Santos's
10. Santos has been quietly making support payments to the woman on behalf of his brother, who is the actual father

S7E15: "Welcome to Wherever You Are"
1. Jon Bon Jovi
2. the clarinet
3. his brother David
4. obstruction of justice
5. Peter Blake, US Attorney for the District of Columbia
6. CJ
7. His ex-wife Andrea (Andy)
8. Halloween
9. Peter Santos, stuffed with ice cream and candy, throws up on a neighbor
10. felon voting

S7E16: "Election Day (Pt. I)"
1. Lester
2. Donna leaves; Josh follows her
3. her career, post-West Wing
4. the exit poll numbers
5. The Foo Fighters
6. thank them for all they've done
7. Kate Harper
8. Leo
9. a massive heart attack

10. Annabeth

S7E17: "Election Day (Pt. II)"
1. "My Cherie Amour"
2. Santos; Lou
3. CJ
4. Santos
5. Santos
6. Vinick
7. Nevada and Oregon
8. He will not exploit Leo's death to challenge a Santos win
9. "Deep in the Heart of Texas"
10. CJ

S7E18: "Requiem"
1. President Bartlet; Abbey; Liz, Ellie, and Zoey; Mallory and her husband; Josh; Donna; Charlie; Debbie Fiderer; Toby; Andy Wyatt; CJ; Danny Concannon; Will; Annabeth; Matt Santos; John Hoynes; Bob Russell; Ainsley Hayes; Amy Gardner; Nancy McNally; Margaret; Carol; Nancy
2. The President, Charlie, Josh, Matt Santos, Barry Goodwin, and Leo's son-in-law
3. Charlie
4. Barry Goodwin
5. English suits; Savile Row
6. apricot
7. Oliver Babish's job – White House Counsel
8. The Hoover Institute
9. Director of Legislative Affairs
10. Bob Russell

S7E19: "Transition"
1. Sam Seaborn
2. "I thought you'd never call!"
3. Deputy Chief of Staff

4. She gives him one month to get his head together about where their relationship is headed
5. Chief of Staff to First Lady Helen Santos
6. Otto
7. China
8. Santo and President Bartlet planned the divergent messages; they are playing Good Cop, Bad Cop with China
9. Lou Thornton; he wants her to take Toby's old job as Director of Communications
10. Donna

S7E20: "The Last Hurrah"
1. Possible schools for their two children
2. that the children will finish out their school year in Houston, meaning their home will need to be Secret Service-fortified (they back away from the decision)
3. which ones she wants to fire
4. to run for president again in 4 years
5. "Ernie"
6. Gov. Eric Baker of Pennsylvania
7. Secretary of State
8. Barry Goodwin, Amy Gardner, and Lou Thornton
9. Barry Goodwin
10. Sheila and Bob, from his campaign

S7E21: "Institutional Memory"
1. She is offered a position running a foundation, funded at $10 billion, to do whatever she thinks is important, by billionaire technologist Frank Hollis
2. President-elect Santos wants her to continue on at the White House as his advisor
3. The DCCC, to be its executive director
4. to unseat a hostile Republican in Oregon's 4th district
5. to ask CJ to speak to the President about pardoning Toby
6. a proposal for an outrageous gas tax
7. a typo in the Constitution

8. She has too many options and doesn't know what she wants
9. Regarding the Hollis job, "That sounds like fun! Does that sound like fun to you?" and "Do you want to work at the White House?"
10. to take the job with Frank Hollis and leave the White House for good; and to pursue a relationship with Danny

S7E22: "Tomorrow"

1. Ronna
2. the framed "Bartlet for America" napkin
3. "WWLD?" (What would Leo do?)
4. Charlie, Will, and Kate
5. Bram
6. signing Toby's pardon
7. Aaron Sorkin
8. "America the Beautiful"
9. Josh, Sam, and Bram
10. "What are you thinking about?" Abbey asks Jed, aboard Air Force One as it flies them home to New Hampshire

Jed Bartlet

See how much you know about Jed Bartlet:

1. What is Jed Bartlet's actual first name?
2. What is his brother's name?
3. Why did President Bartlet go to Notre Dame?
4. Why didn't he pursue his original goal?
5. What vegetable doesn't he like?
6. What is his favorite movie?

Leo McGarry

See how much you know about Leo McGarry:

1. What is Leo's middle name?
2. What city is he from?
3. In what branch of the military did he serve?
4. Where did he go to school?
5. He was treated for addiction to alcohol and Valium in 1993. Where?
6. He served in a previous Presidential cabinet. As what?

Josh Lyman

See how much you know about Josh Lyman:

1. What is Josh's father's name and profession?
2. Where did he do his undergrad studies? His law studies?
3. In law school, he earned a prestigious academic status. What was it?
4. His sister died when he was a child. What was her name?

5. How did she die?
6. What sport did he dream of playing professionally?

CJ Cregg

See how much you know about CJ Cregg:

1. Where is CJ from?
2. How many siblings does she have?
3. She achieved distinction in sports in her youth. What did she do?
4. Where did she attend college and grad school?
5. She has a master's degree in what subject?
6. What was her salary at Triton Day when Leo sent Toby to recruit her for the Bartlet campaign?

Toby Ziegler

See how much you know about Toby Ziegler:

1. Where was Toby born and raised?
2. What is his full name?
3. Besides his brother David, what siblings does he have?
4. How many Yankee games has he attended, on the occasion that he speaks of it?
5. He was raised on three public television classics. What were they?
6. How old did one of his grandfathers live to be?

Sam Seaborn

See how much you know about Sam Seaborn:

1. Where did Sam grow up?
2. What summer camp did he attend as a boy?
3. Where did he go to school (undergrad and law?
4. What organization did he serve as recording secretary in college?
5. What journal did he edit while in law school?
6. In what foreign language is he fluent?

Abbey Bartlet

See how much you know about Abbey Bartlet:

1. Where did she earn her undergraduate degree?
2. Where did she earn her MD?
3. In what medical disciplines is she board-certified?
4. At what medical school is she an adjunct professor?
5. How many generations back was her DAR-qualifying relative?
6. For what other West Wing character did Abbey once babysit?

Charlie Young

See how much you know about Charlie Young:

1. What is Charlie's younger sister's name?
2. Where did he attend high school?
3. Where did he take his college classes?
4. He originally applies for a position at the White House other than the President's body man. What position?

5. What movie franchise does Charlie love, from which the President gifts him a DVD, and what is the DVD?
6. Charlie is like a son to the President, who gives him a family heirloom as a gift one Thanksgiving. What is it?

Donna Moss

See how much you know about Donna Moss:

1. What is Donna's actual first name?
2. Where was she born?
3. Where was she raised?
4. To whom did she lose her virginity, and how old was she?
5. Where did she attend college?
6. In what state does she have family, other than her relatives in Wisconsin?

Mrs. Landingham

See how much you know about Mrs. Landingham:

1. What is Mrs. Landingham's first name?
2. What was her husband's name?
3. What is her position when Jed Bartlet meets her for the first time?
4. What are the names of her twin sons?
5. What became of her sons?
6. She treated Charlie like a nephew, and at her funeral, he gives a reading. What is the reading from?

Will Bailey

See how much you know about Will Bailey:

1. We can guess at the school Will attended from the shirt he's wearing while jogging at Camp David. What school is the shirt from?
2. While running, Will calls out that he only has the legs to run what distance?
3. Where did he go to grad school, and on what scholarship?
4. While in grad school, he was president of what student group?
5. He was a speechwriter for a state-level politician who also appeared on *The West Wing*. Who?
6. Will is an Air Force reserve officer. Who does he work for, in the Air Force?

CHARACTER QUIZ ANSWERS

Jed Bartlet

1. Josiah
2. John
3. He was thinking of becoming a priest
4. He met Abbey
5. Green beans
6. *The Lion in Winter*

Leo McGarry

1. Thomas
2. Chicago
3. The US Air Force
4. University of Michigan
5. Sierra-Tucson
6. Secretary of Labor

Josh Lyman

1. Noah; attorney (litigator and partner at Debevoise and Plimpton)
2. Harvard; Yale
3. He was a Fulbright Scholar
4. Joanie
5. She was trapped in their burning home (Josh, who was younger, escaped)
6. baseball

CJ Cregg

1. Dayton, Ohio
2. two older brothers
3. first female player in Ohio high school history to dunk a basketball
4. Williams College; UC Berkeley
5. Political Science
6. $550,000/yr

Toby Ziegler

1. Brighton Beach, Brooklyn
2. Tobias Zachary Ziegler
3. An undetermined number of older sisters
4. 441
5. *Sesame Street*, *Julia Child*, and *Brideshead Revisited*
6. 96

Sam Seaborn

1. Laguna Beach, California
2. Dungeons & Dragons camp
3. Princeton; Duke
4. The Princeton Gilbert & Sullivan Society
5. The *Duke Law Review*
6. Spanish

Abbey Bartlet

1. St. Mary's College (conjecture; she met Jed Bartlet while he was attending Notre Dame, but it wasn't yet co-ed; St. Mary's was Notre Dame's nearby sister institution)
2. Harvard
3. Internal Medicine; Thoracic Surgery
4. Harvard Medical School
5. 17
6. Amy Gardner

Charlie Young

1. Deana
2. Roosevelt High, in Washington, DC
3. Georgetown University
4. part-time messenger
5. James Bond; *On Her Majesty's Secret Service*
6. a set of carving knives made by Boston silversmith Paul Revere

Donna Moss
1. Donnatella
2. Warroad, Minnesota
3. Madison, Wisconsin
4. Freddy Briggs; 16
5. University of Wisconsin
6. Oklahoma

Mrs. Landingham
1. Dolores
2. Henry
3. secretary to Jed Bartlet's father at the prep school where he was headmaster
4. Andrew and Simon
5. They were killed in a firefight in Da Nang, Vietnam, on Christmas Day, 1970
6. *The Book of Wisdom*

Will Bailey
1. Carnegie Mellon
2. 5 miles
3. Cambridge; a Marshall Scholarship
4. The Cambridge Union Society
5. California Gov. Gabriel Tillman
6. JAG (Judge Advocate General) Corps

The Supreme Court

Match the justice/nominee to what they did/said.

1.	E. Bradford Shelton	a.	said "Voters like guts, and Republicans have got 'em."
2.	Ronald Dreifort	b.	almost but not quite
3.	Christopher Mulready	c.	rulings were upheld by the Court of Appeals more than any other district judge in the country
4.	Joseph Crouch	d.	once snuck a copy of *Lady Chatterly's Lover* out of the public library
5.	Roberto Mendoza	e.	potential nominee; does not take positions on issues
6.	Peyton Cabot Harrison III	f.	is the reason a couple of mixed race can get married in Texas
7.	Evelyn Baker Lang	g.	wrote a book that flushes the doctrine of enumerated rights down the toilet
8.	Roy Ashland	h.	is intolerant toward gays, lesbians, blacks, unions, women, poor people, and the 1st, 4th, 5th, and 9th amendments

Guest Stars

Match the actor to their role on *The West Wing*.

1. Ed Begley, Jr.

2. Tom Skerritt

3. Oliver Platt

4. Christopher Lloyd

5. Glenn Close

6. Laura Dern

7. Janeane Garofolo

8. Mason Adams

9. Nick Searcy

10. John Larouquette

11. Mel Harris

12. Matthew Perry

a. Supreme Court Justice Joseph Crouch

b. SCOTUS nominee Roberto Mendoza

c. Asst. AG nominee Jeff Breckenridge

d. Film mogul Ted Marcus

e. Lord John Marbury

f. White House Council Lionel Tribbey

g. Joey Lucas

h. White House Council Oliver Babish

i. Associate WH Council Joe Quincy

j. Congressman Henry Shallick

k. Senator Seth Gillette

l. Asst. Secretary of State Albie Duncan

13. Carl Lumbly   m. Poet-Laureate Tabitha Fortis

14. Brian Dennehy   n. Chief Justice Evelyn Baker Lang

15. Edward James Olmos   o. Cathy the Indiana farmgirl

16. Corbin Bernsen   p. Marco Arlens

17. Hal Holbrook   q. Sen. Chris Carrick

18. Roger Rees   r. Congressman Nate Singer

19. Amy Adams   s. Prof. Lawrence Lessig

20. Matthew Modine   t. Sen. Ricky Rafferty

21. Bob Balaban   u. Sen. Rafe Framhagen

22. Marlee Matlin   v. Louise (Lou) Thornton

Who said that? (Round 1)

Match the statement with the person who said it.

1. "Nature is to be protected from. Nature, much like a woman, will seduce you with its sights, its scents and its touch. And then it breaks your ankle. Also like a woman."

    a. Toby

2. "I'm in some hellish hold world of holding."

    b. Bruno Gianelli

3. "We're a group. We're a team, from the President and Leo on through. We're a team. We win together, we lose together. We celebrate and we mourn together. And defeats are softened and victories sweeter because we did them together."

    c. CJ

4. "Zippity-do-dah"

    d. Mrs. Landingham

5. Ah, sarcasm – the grumpy man's wit."

    e. Oliver Babish

6. "You're wrong! Just stand there in your wrongness and be wrong!"

    f. Josh

7. "This country is an idea, and one that's lit the world for two centuries!"

    g. Jed Bartlet

8. "I'm gonna crush him, I'm gonna make him cry, and then I'm gonna tell his momma about it!"

    h. Sam

The Bartlet Administration Cabinet

Match the position to the person(s).

1. Roger Tribbey   a. Secretary of State

2. Deborah O'Leary   b. Secretary of Defense
   Bill Fisher

3. Ken Kato   c. Secretary of Veterans Affairs
   Karen Browning

4. Dan Larson   d. Secretary of Commerce
   Alan Fisk

5. Bill Horton   e. Secretary of Labor

6. Mitch Bryce   f. Attorney General

7. Carl Reid   g. Secretary of Treasury
   Jack Buckland

8. Bill Trotter   h. Secretary of Education
   Ben Zaharian
   Gerald Deloit

9. Jason Weaver   i. Secretary of Housing and
   Urban Development

10. Jim Kane   j. Secretary of Energy

11. Miles Hutchinson   k. Secretary of the Interior

12. Lewis Berryhill   l. Secretary of Agriculture

In the Senate

Match each Senator to what they did/said.

1. Chris Carrick

   a. staged a Senate filibuster to get autism research included in a major healthcare bill

2. Steve Gaines

   b. called Toby "a patronizing son of a bitch"

3. Tony Marino

   c. a gun-totin', redneck sonofabitch

4. Ricky Rafferty

   d. has a hollow leg

5. Sam Wilkinson

   e. refused, on principle, to vote in favor of a nuclear test ban treaty after being voted out by his constituents, even though his term had not yet expired

6. Max Lobell

   f. attached an anti-abortion rider to a foreign aid bill, drawing the First Lady's ire

7. Rafe Framhagen

   g. held up a round of military promotions to secure a Pentagon contract for a controversial missile launcher to be built in his home state

8. Clancy Bangart

   h. Republican advocate for Social Security reform

9.	Roland Pierce	i. initiated investigation of a friend of Leo's in the defense industry
10.	Seth Gillette	j. tried to hold up a vote on the federal budget to get a gay marriage ban added
11.	Howard Stackhouse	k. Democrat who briefly entered the presidential race alongside Santos, Russell and Hoynes
12.	Matt Hunt	l. angry over the Bartlet Administration's covert Cuba talks

In the House of Representatives

Match each Congressperson to what they did/said.

1. Matt Skinner

    a. said President Bartlet "might not get out alive" if he visited Cromwell Air Force Base

2. Jack Wooden

    b. leading member of the House black caucus

3. Grant Samuels

    c. makes the claim that one in three White House staffers uses drugs

4. Tom Landis

    d. chairs the Congressional committee that grills Leo during the investigation of a possible White House cover-up of the president's multiple sclerosis

5. Jefferson Wyler

    e. called a racist by HUD Secretary Deborah O'Leary

6. Henry Shallick

    f. dies of pneumonia, leaving behind a wife, a son, two daughters, and eight grandchildren

7. Mark Richardson

    g. agrees with 95% of the Republican platform, but not the part about refusing to recognize gay marriage

8. Peter Lillienfield

    h. Deputy House Majority Whip

9. Joseph Bruno   i. Republican; championed a project to clean up Chesapeake Bay

10. Bertram Coles   j. sold Toby his house

11. Barbara Layton   k. attached a child labor restrictions amendment to a crucial trade bill

12. Christopher Finn   l. went several rounds with Toby and Leo over a tax cut on capital gains

13. Karen Kroft   m. Republican advocate for Social Security reform; voted out of office because of an attack ad written by Josh and Toby

14. Jeff Haffley   n. Republican proposing a tax code amendment to subsidize stay-at-home moms

15. Sam Wendt   o. afraid that the military will close a base in his state

16. Jim Carney   p. declared HPV research studying Puerto Rican sex workers to be "questionable"

17. Jim Hohner   q. House Speaker, Bartlet 2nd term

18. Becky Reeseman   r. was acting President

19. Nate SInger   s. House Speaker, Bartlet 1st term

20. Glen Allen Walken   t. lost her seat; offered Chair of National Parks Service

Who said that? (Round 2)

1.   "'Mothers are standing in front of tanks.' And we're going to go get their backs."

_____

2.   "All through history, no one's wanted either of them."

_____

3.   "With the clothes on their backs, they came through a storm."

_____

4.   "It's the only country left in the world where it's impossible to access the Internet."

_____

5.   "International law has no prohibition against any government, superpower or otherwise, targeting terrorist command and control centers. And Abdul Shareef was a walking command and control center."

_____

6.   "Doesn't this mean we join the league of ordinary nations?"

_____

7.   "That is Saudi Arabia – our partners in peace."

_____

8.   "You really want to reach in and kill them where they live? Keep accepting more than one idea. Makes 'em absolutely crazy!"

_____

9.   "Look at the whole board..."

_____

10.   "Mexico's on fire. Why help them? Because we can."

_____

MATCHING QUIZ ANSWERS

The Supreme Court
1. e
2. h
3. g
4. a
5. c
6. b
7. d
8. f

Guest Stars
1. k
2. q
3. h
4. s
5. n
6. m
7. v
8. a
9. r
10. f
11. t
12. i
13. c
14. u
15. b
16. j
17. l
18. e
19. o
20. p
21. d
22. g

Who Said That? (Round 1)

1. e
2. f
3. a
4. b
5. d
6. g
7. h
8. c

The Bartlet Administration Cabinet

1. l
2. i
3. g
4. f
5. k
6. d
7. e
8. j
9. c
10. h
11. b
12. a

In the Senate

1. g
2. h
3. e
4. k
5. j
6. c
7. l
8. f
9. d
10. b
11. a

12. i

In the House of Representatives
1. g
2. e
3. f
4. i
5. j
6. h
7. b
8. c
9. d
10. a
11. p
12. o
13. t
14. q
15. n
16. m
17. s
18. k
19. l
20. r

Who Said That? (Round 2)
1. President Bartlet
2. Kate Harper
3. President Bartlet
4. CJ
5. Acting President Glen Allen Walken
6. President Bartlet
7. CJ
8. Josh
9. President Bartlet
10. Josh

Just for fun:
Six Degrees of Abbey Bartlet

So Jed met Mrs. Landingham in prep school, where his dad was the headmaster and she was dad's secretary. That makes them the oldest connection in *The West Wing*, predating even his meeting Abbey at Notre Dame.

Jed then met Leo at some point in the next decade, but their friendship began in earnest around 20 years later. Leo was also good friends with Noah Lyman, father of Josh. So Leo knew Josh.

Somewhere in between, Abbey Bartlet babysat for a young Amy Gardner. Where she found time to do that, already having at least one daughter of her own and becoming a surgeon, is anybody's guess.

Josh pulled in Sam, and they clearly had been good friends for years – though Josh went to Harvard and Yale, while Sam went to Duke and Princeton. Maybe they met at Dungeons & Dragons camp.

Leo brought in Toby, and Toby had worked with CJ and convinced Leo she should come on board.

Charlie showed up to be a White House messenger (he had his own bike); and Donna just walked in off the street.

But here's where it gets squirrelly...

Abbey knew Amy from having babysat her; but she (Amy) was also "having quite a bit of sex with Chris", Josh's roommate at either Harvard or Yale. Put another way, Amy was babysat by the wife of the best-friend-to-be of the close friend of Josh's dad.[1]

[1] In Six Degrees of Separation terms, the connections above lead us not to Kevin Bacon, but full circle. Read on...

Or, put another way, Amy was babysat by the wife of the best friend of the old friend of the father of the roommate of her future lover Chris.[2]

That's pushing plausibility *waaaayyy* too far, can't we agree?

But even if we grant this against-the-odds coincidence, we still have some unanswered questions: how did Leo know Toby, so well that he wanted him on the campaign over and above Jed's homeboys and in spite of his love of bourbon? And, if we're parsing coincidences – what are the odds that Leo's top-priority political operative's choice for press secretary had been doinked by the Senate boss of the son of Leo's old friend?

Or, put another way, John Hoynes doinked the press secretary selected by the political operative hired by the best friend of the husband of the woman who babysat the lover of the college roommate of Hoynes' staffer Josh.[3]

Let's get to the bottom of *that*...

---

[2] Abbey -> Amy -> Josh -> Leo -> Jed -> (back to) Abbey,

or

Amy -> Abbey -> Jed -> Leo -> Josh -> (back to) Amy

[3] Leo -> Toby -> CJ -> Hoynes -> Josh -> (back to) Leo,

or

Hoynes -> CJ -> Toby -> Leo -> Jed -> Abbey -> Amy -> Josh -> (back to) Hoynes

About the Author

Scott Robinson is an artificial intelligence designer, social scientist, public speaker and musician, and (of course) a die-hard fan of *The West Wing*. He has also been published in *Rolling Stone* and *The Wall Street Journal*. He can be found at

scott.robinson@glenmillscience.com

Made in the USA
Las Vegas, NV
03 December 2024

12996816R00156